Engaging Anthropology

Engaging Anthropology

The Case for a Public Presence

Thomas Hylland Eriksen

Oxford • New York

First published in 2006 by
Berg
Editorial offices:
1st Floor, Angel Court, 81 St Clements Street, Oxford OX4 1AW, UK
175 Fifth Avenue, New York, NY 10010, USA

Paperback edition reprinted in 2006

Berg is the imprint of Oxford International Publishers Ltd.

Library of Congress Cataloging-in-Publication data
A catalogue record for this book is available from the Library of Congress.

British Library Cataloguing-in-Publication data
A catalogue record for this book is available from the British Library.

ISBN-13 978 1 84520 064 0 (Cloth)
          978 1 84520 065 7 (Paper)

ISBN-10 1 84520 064 0 (Cloth)
          1 84520 065 9 (Paper)

Typeset by JS Typesetting Ltd, Porthcawl, Mid Glamorgan
Printed in Great Britain by the MPG Books Group, Bodmin and King's Lynn

www.bergpublishers.com

In loving memory of Eduardo P. Archetti
(1943–2005)

'Even mud gives the illusion of depth.' (Marshall McLuhan)

'You have nothing to lose but your aitches.' (George Orwell)

Contents

Preface

Anthropology, the study of human cultures and societies, is exceptionally relevant as a tool for understanding the contemporary world, yet it is absent from nearly every important public debate in the Anglophone world. Its lack of visibility is an embarrassment and a challenge.

When, in early summer 2004, the cultural magazine *Prospect* presented its list of the top 100 British public intellectuals, not a single anthropologist was on it. This does not mean that university academics were absent – there were historians, sociologists, philosophers and biologists sprinkled among the broadcasters, essayists and critics. The absence of anthropologists should have had the discipline worried – after all, an important part of the social scientist's job in our societies consists in being worried – but there are good reasons to suspect that few cared much. After all, anthropology, whether it calls itself 'social' or 'cultural', hasn't been very public for some time. In fact, it has almost gone underground in the English-speaking world, 'hibernating in a difficult language', as Adorno said, knowing very well indeed what he was talking about.

This situation is puzzling. Anthropology is about making sense of other people's worlds, translating their experiences and explaining what they are up to, how their societies work and why they believe in whatever it is that they believe in – including their whispered doubts and shouted heresies. Anthropologists have an enormous amount of knowledge about human lives, and most of them know something profound about what it is that makes people different and what makes us all similar. Yet there seems to be a professional reluctance to share this knowledge with a wider readership. Translating from other cultures is what we are paid to do; translating for the benefit of readers outside the in-group seems much less urgent. Anthropological monographs and articles tend to be dense, technical and frankly boring, and in many cases they are preoccupied with details, allowing the larger picture to slip away from sight. Attention to detail is not itself a bad thing; professional specialization and the use of a specialized language may be necessary for knowledge to advance among the initiates, lest we all become journalists.

The problem is that all these fine analytic texts, often brimming with insights and novel angles, rarely build bridges connecting them with the concerns of non-specialists. Also, they are far too rarely supplemented by writings aimed at engaging a wider readership. I have written this book, which tries to show how anthropology could matter to every thinking human being, as a result of several years of mounting frustration. I have spent most of my working hours since my mid-twenties as a practising anthropologist and am familiar with no other profession. I am impressed and often awestruck by the professional determination and intellectual achievements of my colleagues worldwide, yet there is quite clearly something about the way anthropological research is presented that turns almost the entire potential readership off. And it cannot merely be put down to inadequate marketing by publishers or incompetence in the general public. When did you last read a proper page-turner written by an anthropologist? I read a lot of interesting anthropology myself, but would more often than not be hard-pressed to answer the question with confidence.

Young students who come to anthropology tend to have a general interest in 'other cultures'. Very often, they are also motivated by a desire to make the world a slightly better place. The task of anthropology teachers is to make certain their students do not forget these initial sources of motivation – that the onslaught of dry theory and abstract models does not detract from the big issues concerning human life in all its diversity, which fuel the passion necessary to keep the flame burning.

This book is meant for anyone who might be interested in glimpsing what anthropology has to offer, inside and – hopefully – outside the discipline itself, and inevitably it is critical of the way we have dealt with our inherited wealth. The criticism is aimed at institutions rather than individuals; luckily, as social scientists, we are expected to know a thing or two about how to change institutions.

I start with an examination of anthropology's role as a central contributor to Western intellectual life – which it has been in the past, and which it should be at present. I then ask what went wrong and how, and suggest some ways in which the abyss between anthropologists and everybody else could be bridged. I then move on to a more detailed examination of the fraught relationship between anthropological writing and the reading world. Here, I have taken the liberty to include some samples of my own writing for the daily press – they are not to be taken as exemplars to be emulated, but as examples for better or for worse.

A few caveats might be well advised at the outset of what could otherwise appear to be an indecently immodest piece of work. First, this small book does not pretend to be comprehensive in any way. The texts I have singled out for discussion have been chosen for their wider social or intellectual relevance, as representative samples, or simply for their public impact. In most (but not all) cases, other examples could have been used instead.

Secondly, I do not wish to belittle the important applied work carried out by colleagues involved in indigenous rights movements, development work, policy advice, immigrant issues and so on. Of course, anthropology already matters both socially and intellectually, far beyond the confines of the academy, in these and other contexts. My concern here, however, is with the way anthropologists tackle (or ignore) matters of public importance through the media, thereby engaging non-anthropologists to discuss shared concerns, in public, with anthropologists. It is about what the Germans call *Die Öffentlichkeit* or, a tad more tepidly, 'the public sphere' in English.

Thirdly, the book largely (but not exclusively) concentrates on English-language anthropology, using a fair number of Scandinavian counter-examples to illustrate the possible roles of public anthropology. The English language has an unchallenged hegemony in contemporary anthropology, and it dominates publishing, conferences and reading lists on the subject. Actually, publications in other languages nowadays also tend to echo Anglophone anthropology, unlike the situation in the first half of the twentieth century, when non-Anglophone anthropologies followed their own itineraries and agendas. When I was recently doing library research for a book on globalization and anthropology, I was disappointed to find much less local flavour in the Spanish- and German-language anthropologies of globalization than I had expected. They mostly referred to, and discussed, the same Anglophone theories and scholars as everybody else, thereby tacitly acquiescing in their own, unjustly imposed identity as peripheral scholars. Still, had I endeavoured to compare different language communities in anthropology, including those who write and speak in Afrikaans, French or Italian, for example, this book would have been a different one, since engagement with a wider public sphere is sometimes significant among anthropologists who use languages other than English.

This book is also, finally, chiefly concerned with the anthropologist as a writer, to a lesser extent with the anthropologist as talker, and hardly at all with the anthropologist as photographer or film-maker. It is the world of words which is in focus.

The book was written in 2004–2005, but some of the arguments were presented and discussed in seminars at the anthropology departments of University College London, University of Cape Town, Rhodes University, Vrije Universiteit Amsterdam and the University of Western Australia during 2003. I thank everybody involved for inviting and enlightening me. An earlier version of the middle part of Chapter 4 was published in *Anthropology Today* in 2003 (Eriksen 2003) thanks to an initiative by its editor, the excellent non-anthropologist Gustaaf Houtman.

I am also grateful to a great number of people, at the University of Oslo and elsewhere, who have been fellow travellers, guides and speed-bumps on my journey of twenty-odd years among ethnic minorities, ceremonial gift exchanges, structuralist binaries, Marxist orthodoxies and postmodern heresies. I cannot even begin to name them – you know who you are – but someone who has perhaps taught me more than anybody about why anthropology matters, is my former teacher and colleague of fifteen years, Eduardo Archetti, whose unique *mestizaje* of playful enthusiasm and intellectual seriousness eludes description. I am also deeply grateful to Berg's two readers, one of whom has made himself known as Keith Hart, for their devastating criticism of the first draft, combined with unflagging support for the project. Their careful, critical reading of my work went beyond the call of duty and resulted, I hope, in a much improved text. Finally, a heartfelt thanks to Kari, Ole and Amanda for making my non-professional life a worthwhile journey as well.

Oslo, May 2005

As this book was going to press, Eduardo Archetti passed away after a period of illness. He had not read it in manuscript, and I had been especially looking forward to his reactions. He would have laughed and pointed out silly errors, mentioned relevant texts and topics I had ignored, disagreed with bits and discussed the wider implications of some of the better ideas. The loss of Eduardo's laughter, generosity and erudition leaves a terrible void in the lives of everyone who knew him.

(June 2005)

–1–

A Short History of Engagement

Anthropology should have changed the world, yet the subject is almost invisible in the public sphere outside the academy. This is puzzling, since a wide range of urgent issues of great social importance are being raised by anthropologists in original and authoritative ways. Anthropologists should have been at the forefront of public debate about multiculturalism and nationalism, the human aspects of information technology, poverty and economic globalization, human rights issues and questions of collective and individual identification in the Western world, just to mention a few topical areas.

But somehow the anthropologists fail to get their message across. In nearly every country in the world, anthropologists are all but absent from the media and from general intellectual discourse. Their sophisticated perspectives, complex analyses and exciting field material remain unknown to all but the initiates. In fact, whenever anthropologists endeavour to write in a popular vein, they tend to surround themselves with an air of coyness and self-mockery, or they stress that the topic at hand is of such a burning importance that they see no other option than (God forbid) addressing non-anthropologists. Philippe Descola, writing in the context of a French anthropology that has produced popular works of great literary and intellectual value, thus describes his mixed feelings when asked by a publisher to write something about the Jívaro, the Amazonian people he had lived amongst, for a general public (Descola 1996). Retracing the process of writing *Les Lances du Crépuscule* [The Lances of the Twilight], he admits to feeling 'an obscure wish to justify to my peers the project of writing an anthropological book "for the general public"' (1996: 208). He then speculates that the curious reluctance of anthropologists to address general audiences may be caused by an anxiety that the outside world might discover 'the fragility of the scientific precepts' fundamental to the subject. In other words, Descola suggests that it may ultimately be a lack of confidence that has caused the cocooning of anthropology. This view has a lot to recommend it although it is partial, and we'll look at it again below. But first it is necessary to make a brief excursion back in time.

For it was not always thus. Things were in fact going rather well for a long time. The Royal Anthropological Institute in London was founded in 1871 in the spirit of bringing science to the masses, and all over Europe and North America, nineteenth-century anthropology was firmly based in the museums, whose very *raison d'être* consisted in communicating with the general public. It was only in the second half of the twentieth century that the dominant Anglophone traditions in anthropology turned away from a wider readership and began to gaze inwards. Why did this happen?

Of the men generally recognized as the founding fathers of modern anthropology, neither Lewis Henry Morgan, E. B. Tylor nor James Frazer saw themselves as members of a closed clique, but happily and energetically took part in the debates of their time. Morgan, whose work on social evolution and kinship has had lasting effects, was read eagerly by the likes of Friedrich Engels; Charles Darwin borrowed from Tylor, the originator of the modern concept of culture, when he wrote *The Descent of Man*. Frazer, the author of the multi-volume *Golden Bough*, a vast comparative study of myth, was one of the most influential British intellectuals of the early twentieth century, stimulating writers like T. S. Eliot and philosophers such as Ludwig Wittgenstein. Dealing with the large questions of cultural history and human nature, these early generations of anthropologists were part of a broad and colourful intellectual public sphere which included naturalists, historians, archaeologists, philosophers and others who strove to understand humanity's past and present. These anthropologists, lacking an academic training in a subject called 'anthropology', were generalizts and often gentleman-scholars of independent means, who respected no institutional boundaries between university subjects in their quest for knowledge. In their last generation, they included Alfred Haddon, whose keen interest in biology led him to theorise human origins, W. H. R. Rivers, a pioneering cultural historian and an unsung founder of psychological anthropology, and Frazer himself.

Posterity has tended to dismiss these early modern anthropologists as dilettantes and, often inaccurately and unfairly, as speculative armchair theorists (Hart 2003). Tellingly, a leading representative of the next generation of anthropologists, Bronislaw Malinowski, boasted in 1922 that ethnology (or anthropology) had now finally begun to 'put its workshop in order, to forge its proper tools, to start ready for work on its appointed task' (Malinowski 1984 [1922]: xv). Professionalization and specialization were under way, and the stage was set for anthropology's withdrawal, although its ultimate cocooning was still a generation away.

In fact, there is a stark contrast between Malinowski and his generation, and the post-war anthropologists, as regards their willingness to talk across disciplinary boundaries and to the interested lay public. Malinowski himself wrote in popular magazines and gave public lectures on topics of general interest, such as primitive economics and sex. Franz Boas, generally acknowledged as the founder of American cultural anthropology and an important public voice in the anti-racist discourse of his time, debated vigorously in the press, in magazines and journals, and at public meetings. His opponents were those who held that race could account for cultural variation, and in the early twentieth century, they were many and powerful. In France and Germany, similarly, anthropologists were immersed in the issues of their day.

and saw themselves not so much as a distinct intellectual movement as members of a larger public sphere exploring topics of shared interest. There was, by the time of the inter-war years, a growing professional self-awareness by anthropologists, who had sharpened their theoretical tools and purified their field methods; but even the likes of E. E. Evans-Pritchard in Britain and Robert Lowie in the USA had to write their books with professionals and non-professionals alike in mind.

In fact, the inter-war years saw some of the most spectacular successes in the history of anthropological interventions in a wider field. Ruth Benedict's *Patterns of Culture* (1934) was a bestseller in many countries, challenging popular preconceptions about culture and founding a research programme within anthropology at the same time. However, it was Boas' and Benedict's student Margaret Mead who would become the greatest celebrity and bestselling author in the discipline in the twentieth century.

At the time when Mead published her first book, *Coming of Age in Samoa* (1928), fieldwork-based anthropology informed by cultural relativism could credibly present itself as a fresh and exciting approach to human diversity, offering genuinely new insights and provocative truths about possible worlds. As emphasized by Marcus and Fischer (1986), Mead's books showed in powerful ways how anthropology could function as a cultural autocritique, by showing that much of what we tend to take for granted might have been different.

It was cultural relativism's finest hour. Boas could confidently, in his best avuncular style, preface his protégé's debut work as an exemplification of the best that cultural relativism had to offer – simultaneously a distorting mirror and a source of new, exciting knowledge, and ultimately probing deeper than most into the human condition:

> [C]ourtesy, modesty, good manners, conformity to definite ethical standards are universal, but what constitutes courtesy, modesty, good manners, and ethical standards is not universal. It is instructive to know that standards differ in the most unexpected ways. It is still more important to know how the individual reacts to these standards. (Boas in Mead 1977 [1928]: 6)

Mead's books never became classics within anthropology. She was perceived as too superficial in her ethnography, too quick to make sweeping generalizations and, arguably, too *engaged* to be properly scientific. Her uncomplicated, often overtly sentimental prose also had its detractors, as when Evans-Pritchard (1951: 96) described it as 'chatty and feminine', perhaps narrowly escaping allegations of misogyny by associating her style with 'what I call the rustling-of-the-wind-in-the-palm-trees kind of anthropological writing, for which Malinowski set the fashion'. In Europe at least, Mead is scarcely read by students, unlike her contemporaries Malinowski and Evans-Pritchard.

In fact, the mixed reactions to Mead's flowing prose seem to have set a standard for the later reception of popularized and engaged anthropology. As a rule, anthropological texts that become popular with a wider readership rarely receive much credit within the discipline itself.

There can obviously be both good and bad reasons for this sceptical attitude. In her eagerness to present crisp and clear-cut images of her 'alien cultures' for her middle-class American readership, Mead rarely shies away from making sweeping generalizations of at least three kinds: she caricatures her own culture, she turns 'the others' into cardboard cut-outs, and finally, she draws conclusions about the characteristic traits of entire cultures after examining the stories of a few individuals. On the other hand, it can equally well be argued that Mead's intellectual style added a few drops of complexity to the lives of thousands, possibly millions, of middle-class Westerners, and the world may have become a slightly better and more enlightened place as a result. Let the academics' academics discuss the finer points about explanation, interpretation and ethnographic accuracy, one might argue in defence of Mead – and leave the dissemination of the main vision to someone capable of doing the job. Apparently, in *Coming of Age in Samoa*, the comparisons between the Polynesians and the Americans were added by Mead following a suggestion by her publisher (di Leonardo 1998).

Mead wrote her first books at a time when cultural relativism stood for a new and largely untried perspective on the human condition, notwithstanding embryonic cultural relativism in canonical Western thinkers like Pascal and Montaigne; in some versions of intellectual history its ancestry is traced all the way back to Herodotos. As a tool for cultural reform at home, Mead's commonsensical relativist injections proved very powerful indeed, influencing beatniks, hippies and other cultural radicals in the post-war period; and her impact as an antidote to facile biological essentialism in the inter-war years should not be underestimated.

In spite of her reputation as a feminist and a cultural relativist, Mead was not accepted as a fully paid-up member in either camp. Di Leonardo very acerbically, at the end of a lengthy treatment of Mead's work, describes Mead's 'relativism' as 'the self-assured modernist's imperial evaluation of the world's cultural wealth for the "benefit of all"', adding that her views of 'benefits' had, naturally, shifted over the decades (1998: 340). She concludes that Mead 'thought the world was both her natural laboratory and a domain in need of her American tutelage' (1998: 363).

Mead was the best known, but far from the only anthropologist of her generation who easily, and with visible pleasure, translated research materials into engaging prose. Ralph Linton, a master of popularization, wrote volumes of fascinating anthropology and sociology without ever lapsing into jargon. His most famous piece was probably 'One Hundred Per Cent American', first published in *The American Mercury* in 1936 before its inclusion in the author's introductory text, *The Study of Man* (1937).

Featured in the chapter on cultural diffusion, the article was originally written as a subversive comment on tendencies to isolationism and nationalist self-righteousness in the US of the 1930s. Linton sets the tone of his ethnographic vignette by an arresting opening sentence: 'Our solid American citizen awakens in a bed built on a pattern which originated in the Near East but which was modified in Northern Europe before it was transmitted to America' (Linton 1937: 326). Following his 'typical American' through the minutiae of morning routines, buying a newspaper with coins (a Lydian invention), eating his breakfast with a fork (a medieval Italian invention) and a knife made of steel (an Indian alloy), he eventually thanks 'a Hebrew deity in an Indo-European language that he is 100 per cent American' (Linton 1937: 327).

Unlike Mead, who had to describe others' lives vividly and intimately to create a basis for empathy and identification, Linton could safely rely on instant recognition among his readers. While she strives to make the exotic appear familiar, he makes the familiar exotic.

And there were others. Even the evolutionist Leslie White, who mobilized expressions like 'harnessing energy' and a distinction between 'general and specific evolution' in a bid to make anthropology less chatty and more scientific, could often be engaging and provocative (like, incidentally, his student Marshall Sahlins). In an article published in a popular scientific magazine, *The Scientific Monthly*, White (1948) talks about anything from mute consonants to women's skirt lengths and the puzzling absence of polygyny in Western cultures. White, who also once expounded at length about the curious American habit of treating dogs as though they were a kind of human, had a complex argument to make about the insignificance of the individual will and the link between technology and culture. Yet he did it without losing his non-anthropologist readers on the way.

Much of the energy invested into popularized and interdisciplinary anthropology at the time came from a culture war fought on two fronts: against ethnocentric supremacism (our culture is the best; the others are inferior) and against biological determinism (humans should primarily be understood as biological organisms). Both tendencies were powerful ideological forces in the West of the inter-war period. After the war, this changed. Nazism had discredited the notion of race and, through a logically dubious corollary, the notion that humans were biologically determined. Scientists were divided on the matter, but the social and cultural anthropologists were almost unanimous in arguing in favour of the primacy of social and cultural factors.

One of the most important public figures of post-war anthropology – a man whose works are rarely read on anthropology courses – was Ashley Montagu. A defender of the view that humans were shaped by the environment rather than by biological inheritance, Montagu had a decisive influence on UNESCO policies in its early days, and until his death in 1999, he tirelessly wrote polemical tracts against biological determinism. Admittedly, his books could be unexciting, but they were lucid, passionate and important in providing ammunition against biological reductionism.

Montagu's position on race and culture conformed to the Boasian view, but it was enhanced by his background in physical anthropology, and the question he addressed also became a public issue of the first order during and after the war.

Doubtless helped by the Nazi atrocities, but also by advances in human genetics, the social and cultural anthropologists had won a provisional victory in the 'nature–nurture' debate. The conventional wisdom from the 1950s and a few decades on was that humans are primarily conditioned socially; consequently biological factors are less important. At the same time, however, the relativist views which were now firmly a part of the anthropologal teachings became controversial from the moment they were seen to be inconsistent with universal human rights. In a 1947 statement on human rights from the American Anthropological Association (AAA), penned by the widely respected Melville Herskovits, denounced the idea of universal human rights, deeming it ethnocentric (AAA 1947). Instead of this so-called universalism, the AAA defended the idea that every culture had its unique values and its own way of creating the good life.

In the post-war era, therefore, two fundamental tenets of the newly institutionalized discipline of social/cultural anthropology became central to public discourse about the world and its peoples. Instead of capitalizing on this new public importance, anthropology began to withdraw soon after the war.

There are exceptions, some of them very notable, and I shall only mention a few which have made a perceptible public impact. In France, where intellectuals of all kinds routinely interact with the outside world, Claude Lévi-Strauss published *Tristes Tropiques* in 1955, a travelogue and a philosophical treatise about humanity which was received well in almost all quarters. Lévi-Strauss, of course, is recognized as a *maître-penseur*, and through his long professional life, he has intervened quite often with political statements – and he seems to have rather enjoyed his exchanges with non-anthropologists, be they philosophers like Sartre or, more recently, sociobiologists.

A couple of decades after *Tristes Tropiques*, the American anthropologist Marvin Harris published a few books in a popular style, the most famous being *Cannibals and Kings* (1978), which sets forth to explain cultural evolution as a result of the interaction between technological and ecological factors. In Great Britain, by the 1960s Edmund Leach was almost alone in writing for magazines, giving radio lectures and engaging in general intellectual debate. Colin Turnbull wrote two books with a perceptible impact outside of anthropology, *The Forest People* (1961) and the much more controversial *The Mountain People* (1972), both of which were meant to shed light on fundamental aspects of social (dis)integration. The latter was adapted for the stage by Peter Brook. Yet, in the 1980s, the only truly bestselling anthropologist in the UK was Nigel Barley, whose humorous books made fun not only of the anthropologist but also, less easily digestible, of his informants. A few more could have been mentioned, including Akbar Ahmed's important popularizing and critical work on Islam (e.g. Ahmed 1992) and David Maybury-Lewis's work on indigenous peoples, such as *Millennium* (1992). Ernest Gellner's stature as a major public intellectual grew until his untimely death in 1995, but it could be argued that it was chiefly Gellner as philosopher and theorist of nationalism, rather than as anthropologist, who became a household name in intellectual circles around Europe. More recently, Kate Fox's popular books about the anthropology of racing, pub-crawling, flirting and Englishness have enjoyed very good sales and positive reviews in the daily press (as well as, it must in all fairness be said, a few extremely hostile ones). The merits of her books notwithstanding, Fox is an outsider in anthropology; she does not participate in professional meetings or contribute to journals and edited books, and she works at an independent centre of applied social research. *Watching the English* (Fox 2004), a description of 'typically English' forms of behaviour, contains no careful presentation of the data on which generalizations are made, and has little to offer by way of analysis. Fox is more comfortable in discussion with people like Jeremy Paxman and travel writer Bill Bryson than in engaging with anthropologists who have done research in Britain, such as A. P. Cohen, Nigel Rapport or Marilyn Strathern. (The only ethnographer of England who is cited in the book is Daniel Miller.) In its review of the book, *The Daily Express* notes that 'Fox is a social anthropologist, but that does not prevent her from writing like an angel' – while the *New Statesman* denounces the book as 'witless, patronising pap'. One cannot help wondering if Fox's ability to write light-hearted, easily digestible prose is a result of her insulation from university-based anthropological research. If that is the case, both parties should take heed.

This trickle apart – and only a few names have been omitted – the best anthropologists were able to do in order to engage people outside academic circles consisted in writing good textbooks, which is fine, but it is not enough.

The source would appear to have dried out. Or had it? Curiously, debate and theoretical development *within* the discipline flourished. The number of professional anthropologists, and the number of conferences, journals and books published, grew by the year. New intellectual fashions, like structural Marxism, appeared, spread and became obsolete. In the 1970s, women entered the subject on a large scale and introduced new ways of writing anthropology, often with a potential for being widely read.

Anthropology became a popular undergraduate subject in the same period, and a certain degree of anthropological common sense seeped into the public sphere, at the same time as neighbouring disciplines such as religious studies and cultural sociology began to borrow ideas and concepts from anthropology. Scholarly works of great and enduring importance were published from the 1960s to the 1980s: Claude Lévi-Strauss's *La Pensée Sauvage* (1962), Mary Douglas's *Purity and Danger* (1966), Victor Turner's *The Ritual Process* (1969), Fredrik Barth's *Ethnic Groups and Boundaries* (1969), Marshall Sahlins' *Stone Age Economics* (1972), Clifford Geertz's *The Interpretation of Cultures* (1973) and Marilyn Strathern's *The Gender of the Gift* (1988), to mention but a few. Yet, the response from the non-academic world was negligible, and this generation seemed to have no Margaret Mead to take current ideas and run with them. The discipline had become almost self-contained.

However, it would be simplistic to conclude that anthropologists no longer try to communicate outside their discipline. For one thing, many are involved in important interdisciplinary work. For another, many try to break out of the charmed circle of their own discipline. To mention one example, Nancy Scheper-Hughes's award-winning books from Ireland (1979) and Brazil (1992) are well written, experience-near in their approach and skilfully constructed, and have received lavish praise from non-professional reviewers. Keith Hart and Anna Grimshaw's pamphlet series, Prickly Pear Pamphlets (from 1973 to 2001), and its successor series, Prickly Paradigm (since 2002) published by Marshall Sahlins, have brought social engagement and good anthropological scholarship together in a snappy, pointed and occasionally funny form. Neither Marxists nor feminists would be inclined to see themselves as 'socially disengaged' or politically somnambulent. In the twenty-first century, anthropologists like Bruce Kapferer and Jonathan Friedman, Verena Stolcke and Cris Shore write powerful texts about the state and the conflict potential of globalization; and I could go on. There is no lack of social engagement or general intellectual savvy among contemporary anthropologists. Yet they – let's face it – hardly seem to matter to people outside anthropology.

Clifford Geertz, the most widely cited living anthropologist inside and especially outside the discipline, deserves special attention here. Geertz is not only an eloquent writer but an erudite man whose frame of reference extends well beyond anthropology. He is almost universally respected inside the discipline and occasionally contributes essays on anthropological publications to *The New York Review of Books*. Geertz's essays, rich in connotations and references to other intellectuals and artists, must be explained and unpacked to undergraduates for unusual reasons: if they fail to make sense of what he writes, the explanation may be that they have never heard of Croce or are uncertain as to exactly what kind of character Falstaff is, not that they are unfamiliar with the Nayar kinship system or Max Weber's view of Calvinism as the spiritual engine of capitalism. Geertz may be the closest anthropology comes to having its own Stephen Jay Gould (that dazzling humanist science writer), but at the end of the day, Geertz is too coy to come clean as a public intellectual. Although it would hardly cost him two calories to write an interesting essay on female circumcision in the *Atlantic Monthly*, or a piece on Islam in Indonesia for the *New York Times*, he does not do this kind of thing. One can only guess at his reasons; it is nevertheless beyond dispute that he shares this inclination to remain in the academic circles of discourse with almost everybody else in his profession – which is a shame.

Norway is an odd exception here. When the main liberal newspaper, *Dagbladet,* made a list of the ten most important intellectuals of the country in January 2005, followed by ten extensive interviews and a lot of noisy, but ultimately useful debate spilling into other media, three of them were anthropologists (there were none in the jury). To this interesting anomaly we shall have to return later.

Styles of Engagement

There are many possible styles of engagement; there is not just one way of engaging a readership which is neither paid (colleagues) nor forced (students) to read whatever it is that one writes. Marvin Harris's readers are unlikely to overlap significantly with Lévi-Strauss's, and their respective books convey their very different messages in equally different ways. Several styles of presentation, one might say dramaturgies, can be identified, sometimes in combination.

David Sutton (1991), in a discussion of the writer–reader relationship in anthropological writing, examines a clutch of successful popularizers, discussing to what extent they enter into a 'partnership' with their readers. Ashley Montagu, he argues, actively solicits the readers' views and reactions, and prods them to allow his ideas to make a difference in their own life. Marvin Harris's strength, moreover, lies in his holism, his ability to make sense of the world as a whole. The book *Why Nothing Works* (Harris 1987), Sutton says, might as well have been titled 'How Everything Fits'. Harris often presents his topics as *riddles* (two of his books have the word 'riddle' in their subtitle). Closure, Sutton observes, 'is always suspended until the end, when he brings everything together' (Sutton 1991: 97). Finally, Wade Davis, in *The Serpent and the Rainbow* (Davis 1986), appeals to the shared world inhabited by both himself and his readers, avoiding any temptation to step back and watch human worlds only from the outside.

All these three ways of engaging the reader appear to have been effective. But in addition, there exist a variety of other strategies of communication with the outside world, which show the potential efficacy of a public anthropology not only in form, but also in substance.

The Verfremdung *or Defamiliarization.* This technique was used to great effect by Bertold Brecht, and a variant is often utilized in science fiction stories, for example in the novels of Alfred Kroeber's daughter, Ursula Le Guin. Some of J. G. Ballard's novels and short stories, moreover, are set in an England of the near future, where a tendency already noticeable in the present is identified by the author and slightly magnified – holidays in Spain, a fascination with speed and violence, communication via technological means such as telephones – with devastating and shocking results. In anthropology, defamiliarization has been praised as a technique of cultural critique (Marcus and Fischer 1986), and it is sometimes utilized by anthropologists who study their own society. As a younger colleague told me, upon his return from fieldwork in a semi-rural locality not very far from his native Oslo: 'Well, obviously one of the first things I asked them was, "Who do you marry?" My training had told me that it is always important to sort this kind of thing out, and even if they didn't respond immediately, I found out soon enough that they marry within a radius of one hour's travel.'

When, in the 1980s, the Indian anthropologist G. Prakash Reddy was invited to study a Danish village, his primary motivation may not have been to defamiliarize the Danes, but that is how his work was perceived. Notwithstanding the flaws and misunderstandings marring his work, Reddy made a number of observations which could have enabled Danes to see themselves from a new angle. Although his analysis (Reddy 1993) was controversial and hotly debated, it may have had the indirect effect of generating some reflection about the ways Western anthropologists unwittingly defamiliarize the people they study, for example village Indians.

Reddy made a number of interesting observations. On his first day of fieldwork in the Danish village, he asked his interpreter if it would be possible to ring someone's doorbell and ask for a glass of water. He thought this might not just be a way to quench his thirst, but also to get his first informant. Fieldwork began in the middle of a weekday, and the village was completely deserted, much to his dismay. The interpreter, incidentally a fellow anthropologist, explained that they couldn't do that; one simply doesn't knock on strangers' doors and ask for water. Later, Reddy would write about the Danes' odd relationship with their dogs, which they treated better, it seemed, than their old parents who might be tucked away in an old people's home; about the weakness and isolation of the small Danish family and other issues that he saw in relation to his implicit horizon of comparison, the Indian village.

As it turned out, however, most Danes did not enthusiastically allow themselves to be defamiliarized. Reddy's book was given a lukewarm reception among anthropologists and non-anthropologists alike, who felt (largely justifiably, it must be conceded) that he had misrepresented the Danes. Some were scandalized.

Although it was published in both English and Danish, and reviewed in the *American Anthropologist* by Jonathan Schwartz, an American-born anthropologist living in Denmark, *'Danes Are Like That!'* is scarcely known outside the country. The really sad thing, however, is that ethnographies of this kind, where anthropologists from the south study communities in the north, remain rare even after all these years.

In general, the technique of defamiliarization – rendering the familiar exotic – seems to have been more common in mid-twentieth-century anthropology than at present. Linton's 'One Hundred Per Cent American' has been mentioned; another classic, which defends its place in the Anthropology 101 courses where it is still a staple, is Horace Miner's amusing article 'Body ritual among the Nacirema'. The Nacirema, of course, are 'a North American group living in the territory between the Canadian Cree, the Yaqui and Tarahumare of Mexico, and the Carib and Arawak of the Antilles.' Their body rituals involve the use of sacred fonts and potions kept in a chest built into the wall. The rituals are secret and never discussed, even privately, except when children are initiated into their mysteries. The medicine men of the Nacirema have imposing temples, *latipso*, and '[t]he *latipso* ceremonies are so harsh that it is phenomenal that a fair proportion of the really sick natives who enter the temple ever recover' (Miner 1956). What Miner does, apart from parodying exoticizing ethnographic jargon, is to sensitize students to the implicit norms, rules and taboos prevalent in their own society.

One of the messages from anthropology is that nothing is quite what it seems. As Daniel Miller and others have demonstrated, fundamental aspects of human life can be illuminated through studies of modern consumption informed by anthropological perspectives. In *A Theory of Shopping* (1998) and the subsequent *The Dialectics of Shopping* (2001), Miller argues that, contrary to popular opinion, shopping is not a selfish, narcissistic kind of activity. Rather, women shop out of consideration for others, whether they buy things for themselves or for relatives and friends. In Miller's analysis, shopping can be compared to sacrifice, and his analysis is also indebted to Marcel Mauss's celebrated theory of reciprocity, or mutual obligations, as the most fundamental glue of human communities.

None of Miller's highly original texts on shopping are popular in a strict sense, but they fulfil their mission as general statements on modernity by being read outside of anthropology narrowly defined – in business schools, and cultural studies and interdisciplinary study programmes on modern society. They also create a *Verfremdung* effect by positing that in fact, many of our everyday practices can signify *the opposite* of what we may be inclined to believe before we have bothered to find out.

The Cultural Autocritique.   Unlike Linton's vignette, Miner's article on the Nacirema is politically harmless and could scarcely be accused of being 'anti-American' when it was published in the 1950s, even if it makes fun of the American craze for cleanliness. In recent years, there has in fact been a substantial demand for similar self-exoticizing exercises in Scandinavia, where tourist boards, the civil service and even private enterprises solicit the services of anthropologists who are charged with the task of telling them 'what they are *really* like'. (Far more often, they ask consultants, who are more expensive, less knowledgeable and much more 'professional' than anthropologists, to do the same thing.)

A more critical, and much more demanding task, would consist in showing the peculiarities of majority culture in the context of immigration. In most if not all North Atlantic countries, it is virtually taken for granted in the public sphere that immigrants are heavily burdened with culture, while the majority are just ordinary people. One of Mead's great contributions to the public discourse of her time consisted in pointing out not only that the middle-class ways of life typical of Middle America were culturally constructed and historically caused, but also that things her readers took for granted could be changed; that gender relations, values underpinning socialization and all sorts of cultural conventions were in fact different in other societies and therefore scarcely natural. This approach is hailed by Marcus and Fischer (1986) as exemplary, although they – like almost everybody else – have misgivings about the quality of Mead's data, both in Samoa and in the USA. They ask for more nuance and context, for proper ethnography on adolescence in the

USA (rather than unreliable non-ethnographic accounts) and a less one-sided view of either culture. It may well be the case, however, that a public intervention of this kind has to make its point clearly and concisely at the outset, adding nuance on the way. In fact, there is quite a bit of nuance in Mead's account from Samoa, although much of it is buried in endnotes.

The Riddle. The narrative structure behind the 'whodunit' or detective story, the riddle form is a time-honoured and well rehearsed form of storytelling, which makes it no less effective today if placed in the right hands. The author begins with a naive, but difficult question (Why did the Europeans conquer the world? Why is the Indian cow sacred? Why do people everywhere believe in gods? Why does the mother's brother have a special place even in many patrilineal societies?) and then spends the next pages – ten or five hundred, as the case might be – answering it. He, or increasingly she, first brushes away resistance by presenting a few alternative explanations to be discarded as ludicrous or misguided, before embarking on the quest for credible answers. If the answer to the riddle is too obvious at the outset, the genre can degenerate into a just-so story. In that case, it may tell the reader, in the space of a couple of hundred pages, how humanity has moved from a foraging life on the savannah, via horticultural and agricultural forms of subsistence, to a situation where the fortunate worry about their mortgages and watch television, while the unfortunate toil mirthlessly as so many forgotten cogs in the heartless machinery of global capitalism.

The bird's-eye-view necessary for this kind of narrative to work properly is rarely adopted by anthropologists, who usually insist on the primacy of the particular, but the genre has been popular for centuries. A latter-day exponent of this style is the late Marvin Harris. Like a currently very successful non-anthropologist, namely the scientist and popularizer Jared Diamond (1997, 2005), Harris skilfully moves between the vast canvas of human history and the nitty-gritty of local customs, weaving them together with a logic which is invincible, all the accounts balanced, until the moment one confronts them with boring details, counter-examples and alternative interpretations.

Harris's popular books are not simple triumphalist accounts of technological progress. Disliked, ignored or sneered at by most of the anthropologists I know, *Cannibals and Kings* is not devoid of embellishments and has a trace of that inner tension which often distinguishes the excellent work from that which is merely good. Praised by *The Daily Express* as a 'brilliantly argued book', it defends the view, inherited from Julian Steward and Leslie White, that cultural evolution is tantamount to an intensification of technology and resource exploitation. Going further than his mentors, Harris also argues that spiritual beliefs are ultimately caused by factors in the physical environment. The aim is 'to show the relationship between material and spiritual well-being and the cost/benefits of various systems for increasing production and controlling population growth' (Harris 1978: 9). However,

Harris's view is that contemporary industrial civilization does not represent the apex of human progress. Unlike revolutionary writings of Marx, there is no place for a happy end in Harris's undialectical history of intensified production. In fact, like Darwin himself, Harris does not identify evolution with progress, and sees a potential catastrophe in the combined effects of population growth and industrial waste. Noting that prehistorical hunter-gatherers tended to be in better health than the succeeding agriculturalists, and that the life expectancy of an infant in early Victorian England might not compare favourably to the situation 20,000 years earlier, Harris manages to add an ounce of uncertainty to his otherwise linear and unexciting storyline. In a sense, he 'suspends closure to the end', as Sutton (1991) puts it, but since the intelligent reader quickly understands that the answer to all his riddles is likely to be protein, the charm in Harris's version of the anthropological riddle lies in his ability to create surprise at how, at the end of the day, everything has a simple functional explanation.

The Personal Journey.   The philosopher A. R. Louch once infamously intimated that anthropology was just bad travel writing (Louch 1966); just as his near-namesake Edmund Leach once remarked that all anthropologists were failed novelists. Every self-respecting anthropologist would oppose this view and point out, perfectly reasonably, that anthropology raises the issues at hand in a much more accurate way than any travel writer would be able to, that it is by far more systematic and conscientious in its presentation of the events and statements of people that form the basis for generalization, and so on. On the other hand, considering the professional scepticism of many contemporary anthropologists, who eschew the word 'science', relinquish explicit comparison and are disdainful of anything that smacks of human universals, a good travelogue might well pass for an ethnography today. In principle, that is; it does not seem to happen very often in practice.

The scarcity of readable, personal, anthropological travelogues is puzzling. It seems that just as anthropologists excel in the study of other people's rituals but are inept at organizing and immersing themselves in their own rituals, and just as anthropologists have waxed lyrical about 'narratives' for two decades without offering many juicy narratives themselves, all the elements of the personal travelogue are present in the contemporary credo of post-positivist anthropology, yet they are rarely brought to fruition. Contemporary social and cultural anthropology is anti-scientist and concerned with positioning and reflexivity. Phenomenological micro-description and hermeneutic empathy are contemporary virtues. And yet, there remain few bona fide anthropological monographs that have the characteristics of the personal journey. Michel Leiris's *L'Afrique Fantôme* (1934) is one classic example, but it was not thought highly of by his professional peers in Paris. It was too personal and too critical of colonialism in the wrong way, and according to Boskovic (2003: 4), it embarrassed Marcel Griaule sufficiently for him to discontinue all contact with Leiris after its publication.

The one work that stands out, and which is included in any general assessment of the author's œuvre, is Lévi-Strauss's *Tristes Tropiques* (1978a [1955]). The book seems to have no equivalent in English. Even the most personal monographs of recent years in the English language, executed in a spirit of 'experimental writing' (*pace* Marcus and Fischer 1986) and often portraying only a handful of informants, tend to be peppered with jargon and metatheoretical discussions (well, there are admittedly a few exceptions, such as Wikan's *Life Among the Poor in Cairo* (1980), Scheper-Hughes's *Death Without Weeping* (1992) and Davis's *The Serpent and the Rainbow* (1986), but they are rare).

Tristes Tropiques reveals Lévi-Strauss's world-view. It tells us a little about the tenets of structuralism, especially in the passages dealing with Amazon peoples and the autobiographical chapter describing how Lévi-Strauss decided to become an anthropologist. But the message of the book lies in its sad beauty; the textures and sentiments evoked in the unwilling traveller's story overshadow any ethnographic or theoretical merit that it might possess. The book is a travelogue proper; it is long, poorly organized (one might say unstructured), full of prejudice and nostalgia, and it is also deeply engaging. *Tristes Tropiques* was described as 'one of the great books of our century' by Susan Sontag, it moved Geertz to compare Lévi-Strauss with Rousseau, and it was important in bringing structuralism to the attention of the French (and later the Anglo-Saxon) intelligentsia. And it begins with the infamous sentence, 'I hate travelling and explorers'. So much for fieldwork, one might think, until, later on the same page, the author elaborates:

> Adventure has no place in the anthropologist's profession; it is merely one of those unavoidable drawbacks, which detract from his effective work through the incidental loss of weeks or months; there are hours of inaction when the informant is not available; periods of hunger, exhaustion, sickness perhaps; and always the thousand and one dreary tasks which eat away the days to no purpose and reduce dangerous living in the heart of the virgin forest to an imitation of military service... (Lévi-Strauss 1978a [1955]: 15)

This kind of bad-tempered outburst, a reader might be forgiven for thinking, would best have been kept in the notebooks where it had, after all, lingered for fifteen years before the author decided to finish the book. But then Lévi-Strauss goes on to express his ambition to write a different kind of travel book; he freely confesses that he finds it incomprehensible that travel books enjoy such a great popularity, a statement which is intended to make the reader expect that this book is going to be different. The jaded reader, knowing what he can usually expect from travel writing, sharpens his ears. Soon, he is drawn into the universe of the traveller who hates travelling, the ethnographer unable to get into contact with his informants, the anthropologist unable to conceal his contempt for Muslim societies, the travel writer who despises travel writing. Yet Lévi-Strauss manages to pull it off. Like Alan Campbell (1996), I have often wondered why *Tristes Tropiques* became such a success, given its contemptuous attitude and self-defeating tone. Unlike Campbell, I like the book and believe the reason is the enigmatic persona of the writer and the many inevitable tensions that arise between him and his world. When Lévi-Strauss arrives in India, one cannot but wonder how he is going to cope with the filth, the misery and the sheer amorphous mass of Indian culture. (As it turned out, he coped slightly better than V. S. Naipaul would in the early 1960s.) The book drips with nostalgia, it is almost devoid of deliberate humour, most contemporary readers are likely to see the author as dated and prejudiced – and yet the book commands our interest. There is no doubt that Lévi-Strauss is a worthy companion, and he challenges our prejudices (or perhaps our belief that we have shed our prejudices) when, for example, in one of the book's more memorable passages, he says:

> Now that the Polynesian islands have been smothered in concrete and turned into aircraft carriers solidly anchored in the southern seas, when the whole of Asia is beginning to look like a dingy suburb, when shanty towns are spreading across Africa, when civil and military aircraft blight the primeval innocence of the American or Melanesian forests even before destroying their virginity, what else can the so-called escapism of travelling do than confront us with the more unfortunate aspects of our history? (Lévi-Strauss 1978a [1955]: 43)

Now this is quite a mouthful, and it is well worth pondering in the wider context of the book and, especially, the much wider context of an interconnected world. The point is not whether one sympathises with Lévi-Strauss's vision or not (personally, I consider it dangerous and reactionary), but whether he succeeds in bringing anthropology to non-anthropologists. The answer must be affirmative, and the reason is that the book is written in such an insistent, passionate voice that the reader is transported to the Amazon lowlands or the lofty heights of theory, almost without noticing.

The anthropological travelogue, written as a personal journey where the author addresses his readers as fellow travellers, has considerable untapped potential – it exists in France, in books such as Descola's *Lances du Crépuscule* and the series *Terres Humaines*, but in general, it is not established as a respectable genre, as something an academic may do without blushing. On the other hand, it is often mentioned that only small portion of the knowledge that the anthropologist returns with from the field is being effectively used in her articles and monographs. We tell our doctoral students and even MA students, returning from a mere three to six months of fieldwork, that they have to edit their fieldnotes carefully, with their research questions in mind, and leave out everything superfluous or irrelevant. This is a painful thing to do, killing one's babies and leaving one's cherished memories to oblivion, but much could be salvaged through a different kind of text. Perhaps the main explanation is simply that academic education tends to destroy our ability to write well.

The Intervention. It is not difficult to find anthropologists whose work and life are fuelled by a burning moral and political engagement. Many of them do important and admirable work with students, with NGOs and other kinds of organizations; some write important texts about violence, the State, economic exploitation or culture and human rights, just to mention a few topics – but few step forwards to the flickering edges of the limelight in order to intervene in the unpredictable and risky public sphere of the media and general non-fiction ('trade') publishing. Many say that they lack the skills, not the will; but that is no excuse – skills come from practice, and one has to begin somewhere.

Apart from writing well, the most important unlearning that takes place at university affects the students' normative motivations. Time and again, students are being told that it's fine if they want to save the world, but really, academic learning is about understanding it – so if they would please keep their 'ought' to themselves, they can have some more 'is' as a reward. Crude subjective opinion does not belong in a dissertation, which is supposed to be something different from a political tract. While I agree broadly with this view – analytical work is and should be different from advocacy – there is only a short step from neutral description to numbness, and a false contrast is seen to appear between professionalism and engagement. I suspect that not a few anthropologists have lost their original motivation for studying the subject – understanding humanity, or changing the world – on the way, replacing it with the intrinsic values of professionalism. And yet, just as the anthropological travelogue may be complementary to the monograph, the engaged pamphlet can often be a necessary complement to the analytical treatise. However, that pamphlet is written too rarely. It gives you no points in the academic credit system, it may cause embarrassment among colleagues and controversy to be sorted out by oneself. The easy way out, and the solution most beneficial to one's career, consists in limiting oneself to scholarly work. Yet Gerald Berreman was right when, speaking at the height of the Vietnam War, he said that:

> [the] dogma that public issues are beyond the interests or competence of those who study and teach about man comprises myopic and sterile professionalism, and a fear of commitment which is both irresponsible and irrelevant. Its result is to dehumanize the most humanist of the sciences. (Berreman 1968: 847)

In contemporary anthropology, there is one subject area in which the practitioners are unusual in being generally strongly and explicitly engaged, namely the study of indigenous peoples. Organizations such as Cultural Survival and IWGIA (International Work Group of Indigenous Affairs) were founded by anthropologists – the former by David Maybury-Lewis, the latter by Helge Kleivan – and under their auspices, much anthropologically informed policy work and advocacy, popularizations aimed at enlightening the public, and normatively motivated research, is being carried out. The area of indigenous issues is a small universe of its own, shaped in no small degree by anthropologists.

One of the most important anthropologists to devote himself to an openly normative, generalizt project in the twentieth century was Ashley Montagu, whose most famous book, *Man's Most Dangerous Idea: The Fallacy of Race* was first published during the Holocaust, in 1942. Going through several revisions, the sixth updated edition came out in 1997, when the author was ninety-two. Montagu had one big idea, with both academic and political ramifications: that race was a dangerous fiction, and that humans were chiefly social and not biological creatures. The view was uncontroversial in mainstream social and cultural anthropology, and Montagu was never lionized among his own, in spite of his work, spanning more than half a century, which consistently demonstrated the intellectual and political importance of the perspectives drawn from Boasian cultural anthropology.

Although he commanded a great deal of respect and affection, Montagu's books were neither loved nor admired in the way readers might love Mead's books and admire those of Lévi-Strauss. But many recognized them as being important and necessary. Montagu's main shortcoming as a popular writer consisted in not being a storyteller, a lack which would incidentally not have been a problem had he confined himself to the academy. Consider the following, typical extract from a popular article of his:

> In view of the fact that there exists, at the present time, a widespread belief in the innate nature of competition, that is to say, that competition is a form of behaviour with which every organizm is born, and that this is particularly true of man, it will be necessary to discuss such facts, with which scientific studies have recently acquainted us, which throw light upon this notion.
>
> Just when the idea of the innate competitiveness of man came into being I have not the least idea. It is at least several thousand years old, and was probably in circulation long before the Old Testament came to be written. It is quite possible that the idea of the innate competitiveness of man is as old as man himself. There are some existing non-literate cultures, such as the Zuni of the American south-west, which abhor competition and in which the idea of innate competitiveness is non-existent. It is quite possible that many prehistoric peoples held similar notions. (Montagu 1952)

Lucid and informative? Definitely. But engaging and exciting? Hardly. Yet it must be kept in mind that Montagu, a British Jew himself, studied under Boas at a time when mainstream intellectuals and politicians saw eugenics as reasonable and racial science as respectable, and that he wrote his first major book about race and culture at the height of the Second World War. The time and topic placed the context of his work beyond the demands of the entertainment industry.

The Essay. This challenging literary genre can be defined as an extremely sub-jective form of non-fiction. Assuming that Leach was right in claiming that most anthropologists were failed novelists, here is a chance to become a truly creative writer without having to invent persons and events. Michel de Montaigne, the sixteenth-century thinker usually credited with the invention of the literary essay, saw his texts as *essais* in the proper sense of the word, that is, as *attempts*. The essay, unlike the article, is inconclusive. It plays with ideas, juxtaposing them, trying them out, discarding some ideas on the way, following others to their logical conclusion. In the celebrated climax of his essay on cannibalism, Montaigne forces himself to admit that had he himself grown up among cannibals, he would in all likelihood have become a cannibal himself. This is not an option that most sixteenth-century French noblemen would have even contemplated.

It is possible to place essays on a continuum between the literary essay, verging on prose-poetry at one extreme, and the non-literary, which at the other extreme approaches the article or non-fiction book. Unlike other non-fiction genres, however, the essay has to be written in a spirit of exploration. The author must not give the impression that she knows all the answers before the writing process begins (even if she thinks she does). Moreover, in the essay, the writer sees the reader as an ally and companion, not as an antagonist to be defeated or persuaded. The essay appeals to the reader's common sense, it may occasionally address him directly, and the essayist tries to ensure that the reader follows her out on whichever limb she is heading for.

There are many splendid examples of anthropological essays. Many of Geertz's celebrated writings would fit most of the criteria. Books such as Adam Kuper's *Culture: The Anthropologist's Account* (1999) and possibly Mary Douglas's *Purity and Danger* (1966) could be classified as essays. Pierre Clastres's remarkable *La Société Contre l'État* (1977; *Society Against the State*, 1988) is both a romantic travelogue, a critical intervention with an anarchist tendency and – chiefly – an essay about the fate of stateless peoples in the modern world, written in the tradition of Leiris and Caillois. The German maverick anthropologist Hans Peter Duerr, through his bold criticism of Norbert Elias's theory of 'the civilizing process' and his somewhat New Age tinged account of shamanism (Duerr 1984), has also engaged with the general intellectual debate of his time through the demanding, open-ended form of the learned essay. There are also some others – but again, they are surprisingly few. Rather than appealing to common sense and intellectual curiosity in the reader, most anthropologists close themselves off from general scrutiny (and readership) by retreating into the arcane conventions of the discipline.

One anthropologist who did not succumb to this temptation was Ruth Benedict, who wrote one of the most influential books about Japanese culture during the Second World War. The book's success may have led to some professional embarrassment among those who saw hands-on fieldwork *sur place* as the only possible way of gaining insight into another culture, since Benedict had never been to Japan, nor did she speak or read Japanese. Unlike the other American academics enlisted by the US Office of War Information to make sense of the enemy, however, she met and interviewed many Japanese who were interned in the USA, watched Japanese films and discussed them with natives, and did everything in her power to obtain intimate knowledge of that 'enigmatic culture' from a distance (Hendry 1996).

Some readers may be surprised to find Benedict's *The Chrysanthemum and the Sword* as an exemplar of the anthropological essay. For was it not a book commissioned by the war industry, written with a very clear objective in mind, namely to understand the Japanese in order to defeat them? And did not Benedict also embody the very opposite spirit to that of the good essayist: linear, abstract, confident in her own answers? Well, yes, but her book on Japan is very different from the commercially much more successful *Patterns of Culture* in that she approaches her subject matter with a certain humility and bewilderment, allowing her readers to share her initial confusion. The book, written largely for non-anthropologists, actually influenced not only policies during the post-war American occupation of Japan (a later version of the US government might have needed a similar book on Iraq), but has also led to vivid debates about Japanese culture and identity in Japan itself. According to a source cited by Hendry (1996), the book may have been read by as many as twenty million Japanese! The book is written and composed in the riddle genre, interspersing analysis and description with doubt and uncertainty. In the end, everything seems to fall neatly in place, but the book is sufficiently ambiguous (a virtue in essay writing; a vice in standard academic practice) to have been read in many ways, almost like a work of literature. Now, many recent anthropology books are also interpreted in different ways, but the reason may just as well be obscurity, deliberate or involuntary, as complexity – and obscurity is not to be conflated with subtlety. In Benedict's case, there is little of the former but much more of the latter.

The Biography.   Single-informant ethnographies exist, such as Crapanzano's *Tuhami* or Shostak's *Nisa*, and many 'whole society' ethnographies might have been written as biographies, relying as they do on key informants. Add to this the growing appreciation of the life story as empirical material in anthropology, and it becomes nothing short of puzzling that so few anthropologists have written accessible, engaging biographies of people they know intimately. Publishers want biographies, readers want biographies, and the best biographies portray a time and a place just as much as they tell the life story of some individual deemed interesting for one reason or another.

Life stories have been put to several interesting uses in recent years. One method is that deployed by Marianne Gullestad in *Everyday Philosophers* (1996), where the informants have themselves written lengthy narratives about their own lives and the anthropologist assumes an editor's role. Although few would use this method in its extreme form, prompting informants to write about themselves is arguably an underused form of data collection. A less experimental, but no less successful, method is the one employed by Katy Gardner in *Songs from River's Edge* (1997), surely one of the most beautifully written ethnographies of recent decades. Based on village fieldwork in Bangladesh, Gardner's book has in effect crossed the boundary into literature, and it is presented by the publisher as a collection of stories. (She also published a more academic book from the same fieldwork.) Gardner has chosen narrative over analysis, and the book is free of jargon and was published as a trade book, not as an academic monograph. Reading it made me think that there is no good reason why anthropologists should not combine this approach – let the people's biographies and the events the anthropologist encounters speak for themselves – with an analytical wrapping at the beginning and the end. This is not the place to discuss whether Gardner's unusual way of presenting her ethnography is useful for anthropology (I suspect it might be, but there are several issues that need to be addressed before concluding), but as a way of enlarging a general readership's vision of the world, it is commendable. A flourishing of well-written anthropological biographies, or documentary stories, would doubtless raise anthropology's presence in the popular consciousness, and as an additional bonus, it would alert the public to the differences between anthropology and other forms of academic inquiry such as cultural studies.

Just before the final deadline for this book, a new sub-genre of the anthropological genre was introduced by Alan Macfarlane, a Cambridge professor chiefly known for his studies in cultural history. Macfarlane's *Letters to Lily* (2005) consists of thirty thought-provoking letters to his granddaughter, where he imagines her to be around seventeen (at the time of writing, she is seven). The letters are anthropologically informed responses to questions Macfarlane assumes she will ask, such as: Why is there war? What is love? Where does freedom come from? A kind of anthropological *Sophie's World*, the book is a splendid demonstration of anthropology's ability to function as an empirically based philosophy, which has important things to say to anyone who is uncertain of where she, her society or indeed the world is heading. Rather than offering answers, Macfarlane invites the reader to linger near the questions.

Since the Second World War, anthropology has shrunk away from the public eye in almost every country where it has an academic presence. Student numbers grow; young men and women are still being seduced by the intellectual magic of anthropology, ideas originating in anthropology become part of an everyday cultural reflexivity – and yet, the subject is all but invisible outside its own circles. In fact, one of the greatest anthropological publishing successes of recent decades has been something of an embarrassment to the subject, namely Nigel Barley's satirical books from Central Africa and South-East Asia (Barley 1985). The feeling that anthropologists feed in a parasitical manner on 'the others' is still rather widespread among intellectuals outside the discipline, and Barley's books have done little to disprove this view.

With few exceptions, the examples of successful public engagement that I have discussed above were published at least half a century ago. Paradoxically, as the discipline has grown, its perceived wider relevance has diminished. In the mid-twentieth century, the day of Mead, Montagu and Evans-Pritchard, anthropologists still engaged in general intellectual debate and occasionally wrote popular, yet intellectually challenging, texts. The number of anthropologists doing so has dwindled. In the USA, William Beeman may be alone in writing regularly for the press, and the cultural anthropologists visible in the huge and variegated American media landscape – Nancy Scheper-Hughes and Micaela di Leonardo are among them – can easily be counted. In the UK, Edmund Leach (d. 1989) and Ernest Gellner (d. 1995) were the last major public intellectuals among anthropologists.

There are more of us than ever before, yet fewer reach out to communicate with a wider world. Probably there is a cause and effect here. As Jeremy MacClancy has remarked (1996: 10; see also Grimshaw and Hart 1993, Wilken 1994), the number of professional anthropologists was so limited in the inter-war years that monograph writers were forced to keep a general educated audience in mind as they wrote. After the Second World War, anthropologists have increasingly been talking to each other, the argument goes, simply because they no longer had to speak to others.

As a general explanation this will not do. Surely, there is a very significant number of historians in the Anglophone world as well, yet many of them are extremely successful in their attempts to communicate with non-historians. Their professional community is less sequestered, less bounded, less smug and possibly less self-righteous than the anthropologists' guild. There is something that the historians do that anthropologists could learn from.

An anecdote about the historian and the anthropologist may give a hint. The historian and the anthropologist discuss the relative merits of their subjects. The anthropologist says, in a smug voice: 'Well, if you historians intend to study a river, you have to wait until it has dried out. You then enter the dry riverbed with your magnifying glasses and whatnot. We anthropologists, on the other hand, wade straight into the messy wetness of the river and stay there until we have been able to make sense of it as it flows by.' The historian lights his pipe, looks out of the window and answers slowly: 'Yes, I suppose you are right. Yet, you anthropologists seem to dry out the living river, while we historians endeavour to bring water to the dry riverbed.'

What historians do is to tell stories. What anthropologists do is to convert stories into analysis. While this brings us a little closer to answering the question of why anthropology is out of touch with the popular consciousness, the question is sufficiently complex, and has enough ramifications, to need a chapter of its own.

–2–

What Went Wrong?

The withdrawal of anthropology from general intellectual discourse in the latter half of the twentieth century is a fact which needs no further qualification. There are important exceptions – some have been mentioned already, while others will be discussed later – but on the whole, anthropological discourse has withdrawn into itself. In trying to account for this tendency and criticizing it, it is not my intention to belittle, in a spirit of anti-intellectual populism, the significance of academic anthropology, nor am I oblivious to the wide-ranging and highly consequential practical and applied work carried out by anthropologists who function as critics or specialists working with indigenous affairs, 'development aid', immigrants or other social issues. The question I am raising is simply why it is that contemporary anthropologists are so reluctant to present their work to larger audiences inside and outside the academy, and why it is so important that we do so.

There are many possible scapegoats. The last decades of the twentieth century saw a fundamental transformation of – in descending order of importance – the universities, the role of the academic intellectual in society, and anthropology. Universities are being turned into factories. Academics have, as a consequence, lost much of the time they could formerly devote to engagement in greater society, they have been specialized to the point of fragmentation and besides, their societal authority has diminished. As far as anthropology is concerned, the grand theories where everything could be made to fit evaporated around 1980, Third World liberation made the classic anthropologist seem to be a neo-colonial romantic refusing locals the right to define themselves; and the assault of postmodernism on any kind of truth claim was the last thing anthropology needed, saturated as it already was with self-doubt.

Perhaps non-engagement or aloofness from social issues is the main residue of the old cultural relativism, that is the spirit of letting the natives deal with native problems? Or perhaps the misuse of the culture concept in ethnic conflicts and nationalist wars has given us cold feet? There are many possible interpretations. Yet anthropology is, or should be, particularly relevant in the contemporary world, as a way of thinking comparatively, based on a local perspective on human affairs.

The Art of Staying Aloof

The position of academics in greater society varies. In Norway, anthropologists are routinely contacted by organizations and media, asked about their opinions or invited to give public talks on some topic of general interest. This is not the case, for example, in the USA. A few years ago, on a visit to Norway, Michael Herzfeld mentioned that he would like to reach a greater audience with his work, but alas – anthropology books sold poorly. Fredrik Barth suggested that he give a few talks to associations or organizations outside the university, in order to get to know his potential readership better. Herzfeld saw the proposition as being entirely unrealistic. How on earth should he get in contact with such associations? (Gullestad 2003).

In some countries, there are many possible lines of communication connecting academics with 'the outside world'; in others, these lines seem to be absent for all except a handful of authorized public intellectuals. This difference may have something to do with scale and differentiation; the number of media outlets, both fast and slow, is generally much higher per capita in a small, rich country than in a large country, rich or poor. Oslo has nine newspapers for a population of less than a million. Perth has one, the *West Australian*, for a population of a million and a half. Yet in spite of such objective factors, it can hardly be denied that to some extent, the isolation is self-imposed. There is much unpleasant, if invisible and implicit, boundary-patrolling taking place in anthropology departments around the world. Anthropologists justly pride themselves on their strong group identity as a profession, but the downside of any strong, proud group identity is – as every anthropologist knows – a glorification of one's own achievements at the expense of denigrating those of others. We sometimes behave as though anyone who makes a comment on, say, child labour in Pakistan, and who hasn't done lots of fieldwork there, is not to be taken seriously. This is a preposterous and unproductive attitude. It is time to admit that the diffusionist Elliot Smith was not entirely off the mark when he wrote, in a private comment on Malinowski, that he failed to understand that 'the sole method of studying mankind is to sit on a Melanesian island for a couple of years and listen to the gossip of the villagers' (Elliot Smith quoted in Stocking 1992: 58). Again, this should not be understood as a negative view of the ethnographic method, only as a reminder that there may exist different sources of valid knowledge.

Several books published since the early 1980s have taken issue with the apparent irrelevance of anthropology to the outside world. One of the most influential has been the aforementioned *Anthropology as Cultural Critique* (Marcus and Fischer 1986), where the central argument is that anthropology in the late twentieth century had the potential to repeat some of the popular and critical successes of the interwar years. Since its subject matter had become ever more complex, and because of relevant criticism by feminists, former colonial subjects and others, anthropology was going through 'an experimental moment' which ought to have, in the view of the authors, inspired anthropologists to use their knowledge of other cultures to question basic assumptions in their own. To some extent, this has come about in the intervening two decades, but this development has had no direct effect on the relationship between anthropology and the non-academic world of public discourse, although it is possible, as Benthall (2002a: 4) maintains, that there is a 'trickle-down into public debate'.

Although its message is that anthropology ought to make a difference outside the universities, *Anthropology as Cultural Critique* and ensuing works by the same authors and their associates give no indication of an earnest attempt to convey anthropological insights to the general reader. In that book, and to an even greater extent in *Writing Culture* (Clifford and Marcus 1986), published simultaneously, there is a deep concern with style and rhetoric, with representation (and its so-called crisis) and symbolic power. While this heightened self-reflection has been very tangible in much later anthropology, it cannot be argued that anthropology has made itself more indispensable as a source of cultural criticism in the same period. In fact, the tendency towards cocooning and self-imposed ghettoization was, if anything, even stronger in the 1980s and 1990s than in the previous decades, partly as a result of the weakened position of Marxist approaches to 'underdevelopment', a weakened engagement with issues of global development as a result, and the narcissist temptations of postmodernism. It seems that the much-discussed crisis of representation is really neither more nor less than a crisis of communication.

In fact, in retrospect it is easy to see that postmodernism did considerable damage to anthropology. Other disciplines needed it – mainstream political science is still waiting for its injection – as an aid to develop critical self-awareness and theoretical modesty. In anthropology, debates had already been running for decades about the possibility of translation between one culture and another, the possibility of comparison and issues pertaining to reflexivity and objectivity in description and analysis. With the influx of postmodern ideas (or ideas believed to be postmodern by anthropologists – sometimes Foucault was lumped with Lyotard and Deleuze as 'postmodern') into anthropological writing, the subject got an extra dose of a foul-tasting medicine it had already been struggling to swallow for the best part of a century. Although postmodernism was vigorously resisted – Geertz diagnosed its adepts as suffering from epistemological hypochondria – it made deep inroads into the already fragile self-confidence of anthropology as a robust and scientific way of knowing. A double positive seems to have made a negative in this respect, and the postmodern impulse chased anthropology further down the road of introverted rumination. In a comparison between the romantic Lévi-Straussian Pierre Clastres and the postmodernist historian of anthropology James Clifford, Geertz (1998) concludes that whatever the flaws of his approach, Clastres 'knew where he was going, and he got there.' Clifford, in *Routes*, a book about travel, movement and ethnography, on the contrary 'seems stalled, unsteady, fumbling for direction', and his text has 'a hesitant, stuttering quality (what can I say? how can I say it? with what right do I do so?)'. Postmodernism taught a generation of anthropologists to dissect the menu without bothering to look at the food; it concentrates on the wallpaper patterns instead of the quality of the mason's work.

Cocooning also has a social dimension, which may be peculiar to anthropology. One of the first questions an anthropologist is likely to ask a younger colleague, after establishing his or her field of study, is: 'Who are you working with?', or 'Who was your supervisor?' There are lineages and clans, feuds and old antagonisms enough for everyone. Conflicts tend to be inherited, sometimes for more than a generation. The diplomatic and easy-going Raymond Firth excepted, the relationship between Malinowski's students and Radcliffe-Brown's students seems to have been strained until well into the 1960s (Kuper 1996). In the USA, you were either with Boas or with the dark forces. The sociology of anthropological cliques, loyalties and enmities might, at critical, defining moments in our past, reveal a close family resemblance to the study of religious cults, paranoid or otherwise.

In the previous chapter, some explanations for the cocooning of anthropology were mentioned almost in passing. It is now time to look more systematically at the causes.

Recipes for Cocooning

Elitism

Anthropology, unlike some other academic disciplines, has yet to escape fully from the mouldy lounges and pompous hallways of pre-war university life. In spite of the demographic explosion it has gone through since the Second World War, and in spite of the democratization of higher education, anthropology somehow remains an elite subject in the English-speaking world. Since anthropology is a subject which prides itself on studying the world 'from below', seeing the world 'from the native's point of view', giving voice to 'muted' groups and so on, there is a sad irony in this self-imposed snobbery. In the pioneering days of the early twentieth century, many significant anthropologists were Jews, immigrants and women and were thus, by virtue of personal experience, in a privileged position to understand and empathize with the disenfranchised. They nevertheless tended to have a background in the European cultural bourgeoisie. Mead and Benedict, too, came from solid middle-class backgrounds. But so did most academics regardless of subject, and the early predominance of minorities and women at the very centre of the discipline was significant.

Evans-Pritchard's generation did not even want anthropology to be taught as an undergraduate subject. In Britain, the subject remains dominated by the departments of the elite universities, while the sexier cultural studies ('anthropology without the pain', as a colleague calls it) departments tend to be located in less prestigious red-brick universities. The situation is comparable although sometimes less stark in other countries. When I was recently invited to spend a term teaching at a South African university, I was naively looking forward to meeting an unfamiliar and challenging kind of student. I envisioned the lecture room as thick with the adrenaline of angry young men and women who had suffered at the hands of a theory of culture, apartheid that is, which drew much of its inspiration from early twentieth-century anthropology. The actual anthropology students turned out to be pretty much like the ones I knew from home: pale-skinned, mostly female students from respectable families, whose parents could afford to let their children study a useless subject.

The proper view of anthropology in undergraduate courses should in fact be the opposite of the twentieth-century British elite view: in an ideal world, everybody would take a few courses of anthropology. It is as essential a tool as Plato and Kant for an understanding of the human world.

Some years ago, I asked a British colleague, who now worked in a non-anthropology department, how she felt about not working as an anthropologist proper any more. Slightly annoyed by the question, she said with great emphasis that she was relieved to have left anthropology, maintaining that social anthropology, at least in the UK, was incredibly snobbish, resolutely turning its nose up at anything smacking of populism or 'not proper anthropology', and saturated with an ancient Oxbridge spirit totally out of tune with the contemporary world. The media are regarded with a great amount of condescension, she intimated, and popularization and 'impure' engagements with the outside world (which might compromise one's integrity as one of the selected few) were viewed with deep suspicion.

These remarks led me to recall the situation in Norway, where social anthropology has enjoyed a reputation as an anti-elitist kind of activity – an unruly, anarchist science of greatcoated, ruffled men with unpolished shoes and strange views – since the mid-twentieth century. In the view of many non-academic observers, view it compares favourably with the humanities, where the Western canonical traditions still tend to be reproduced in an almost monastic way, and even with subjects like sociology, where the reverence for ancestors like Weber and Durkheim ('the classics') can sometimes make lectures sound like sermons. Norwegian journalists contact anthropologists for comments on current affairs every day of the week – be it a royal wedding, a sport scandal or recent political changes in a Third World country – and the anthropologists play a not negligible part in public debate.

However, what struck me at the time of the conversation was not this difference, but the fact that although many Norwegian anthropologists now study aspects of their own society, the vast majority of us know much more about contemporary African witchcraft and sacrifice in eastern Indonesia than about the way of life typical of the domestic working class, which could easily be observed a twenty-minute tube ride from the leafy bourgeois environment of the university campus. No anthropologist had stepped forward and tried to explain, on the basis of ethnographic research, why, for example, a substantial part of the working class had recently changed its political alignment from the Labour Party to the populist, anti-immigration Progress Party.

The fact is that there is a certain otherworldliness about academic anthropology, virtually everywhere. Therein lies its charm for the wider public, perhaps. While a sociologist or political scientist might deal with, say, the Olympic Games in terms of the global economy, power abuse in the IOC or domestic nationalism, an anthropologist would be more likely to see it in the light of Western individualism and the cult of modernity, and would presumably interpret it as a ritual, drawing on a century of research on rituals in non-literate societies. Anthropology can offer slanted and skewed, unexpected and thought-provoking perspectives on apparently pedestrian and mundane matters. This has made some anthropologists darlings of the media in Norway, but the very same quality of the subject has led its practitioners to withdraw elsewhere. To put it differently: in spite of its considerable growth, anthropology still cultivates its self-identity as a counter-culture, its members belonging to a kind of secret society whose initiates possess exclusive keys for understanding, indispensable for making sense of the world, but alas, largely inaccessible to outsiders.

Jonathan Spencer (2000), in a partly experience-based account of British anthropology in its main period of demographic expansion, from the 1960s to the 1980s, points out that the dominant figures of the discipline shuddered at the thought of introducing anthropology in secondary schools (see also Shore 1996). Leach argued: 'It could be very confusing to learn about other people's moral values before you have confident understanding of your own' (Leach 1973 quoted in Spencer 2000: 3). As a result of the anthropologists' refusal to adapt their subject to the requirements of A levels, thousands of young Britons have learnt the rudiments of sociology and psychology in their late teens, while hardly anybody has been exposed to anthropology.

The anthropologists simply did not want their subject to become too popular. Fearing the influx of former colonial officers and young idealists who were interested in applying anthropology to non-academic pursuits, the establishment reacted by purifying the subject even further. At the main British universities there were no curricula, but instead very extensive reading lists. Textbooks were rarely used. Again, Leach expressed a dominant sentiment when he stated:

> It must be emphasized to such potential students [who were interested in non-academic employment] that the prospects of ever being employed as a professional social anthropologists (*sic*) are extremely small... I would personally be horrified if it became apparent that the 'syllabus design' ... was slanted towards 'applied anthropology'. (Leach quoted in Spencer 2000: 7)

In the USA, the causes of the diminished engagement with the outside world differed. For one thing, anthropology has always been much larger, both thematically and in terms of demography, in the USA than in any European country. The Association of Social Anthropologists in the UK has a membership of slightly over 500, while the

American Anthropological Association has nearly 12,000 members (Mills 2003: 13). In other words, although the population of the US is only six times that of Britain, there are twenty-four times as many organized anthropologists.

Yet anthropology fails to make significant inroads in the general intellectual discourse on the other side of the Atlantic as well. Popularization and refraining from minding one's own professional business are not activities that add to one's academic credentials. In a situation with fierce competition for few jobs, it pays more to write journal articles in the style of one's teachers than to popularize or enter into general discussions with non-colleagues. More generally, there is a deep abyss between academics and the general public in the US and, as argued by Russell Jacoby (1987), there nowadays seem to be few public spaces available for American intellectuals outside the academy itself.

The Myopic Specialization Resulting from 'my Ethnography'. It could also be the case that the long-term effects of the Malinowskian fieldwork revolution and Boas's historical particularism, together with the new constraints imposed by the post-colonial critique and the increased demand for reflexivity, has made it difficult for anthropologists to retain their professional virtue and simultaneously offer wide-ranging overviews of any kind. The Malinowskian glorification of the detailed, synchronic single-society study encourages specialization and gives the highest marks to the colleague who remains loyal to her fieldnotes throughout her career. It is generally agreed among the majority of English-speaking anthropologists that Radcliffe-Brown, with his futile ambitions for a 'real science' of systematic comparison and cumulative growth in knowledge, is best forgotten; that G. P. Murdock's enormous ethnographic atlas, known as the Human Relations Area Files, is largely useless because the data are decontextualized; and it can also be argued that Jack Goody's ambitious forays into comparative Euro-Asian history are forgiven only because Goody is also an eminent West Africanist. The smaller, the better, in a sense. There is much to be said for such judgements, at least when they are passed in a polemic context. But impure compromises between one's own ethnography and other kinds of knowledge are possible (and are, evidently, made all the time). It may be that the tendency to crawl on all fours with a magnifying glass, rather than circling the world in a helicopter looking at societies with a pair of binoculars, could be anthropology's great gift to the world, but it needs to be supplemented by bold comparisons and sweeping overviews.

Complexity as Conclusion rather than Premise. Some years ago, on a mad drive from Heathrow to Hull, I happened to hear a radio debate about human evolution on the BBC. One of the panellists, an evolutionary psychologist, explained how culture could be seen as part of the human evolutionary process, presenting a theory-of-games kind of model accounting for adaptive advantages. The other participant, a social anthropologist, said something to the effect that, 'Yes, this is probably correct as far as it goes, but we must keep in mind that it is more complex than that.' Of course he was right, but it would most likely be the evolutionist's simple and robust arguments that were remembered by the listeners.

This kind of debate always brings to mind a cartoon, in all likelihood non-existent, which depicts a public demonstration consisting of a large crowd of anthropologists carrying placards and banners with texts such as 'More complexity now!', 'Ambiguity rules', 'Down with simple answers!' and so on.

That is where our predicament lies: what anthropology has to offer appears to be irreducible complexity and ambiguity; in other words, apparently non-marketable commodities with respect to the mass media and the general reader. This is not to say that the reading public is necessarily dismissive of complexity as such, but that most readers expect a book to make sense of the complexity and not just leave the job to the reader. Most anthropologists are reluctant to simplify their insights, and even if they wanted to, it might not always be possible to distil the complexity into punchlines or persuasive arguments neatly wrapping up the preceding chaos. Few monographs or even articles have a simple point to make, one that might be summarized in a single sentence. Some of the popularizing successes of anthropology do make such simple points, which may be a main reason that they are so unpopular inside the discipline: Mead argued that nurture was more important than nature; Harris argued that ecological and technological factors explained culture and society; Turnbull described, in his Mbuti book, an almost Rousseauian state of Eden, and so on. The practising ethnographer is sceptical of such books, and with sound reasons, at least if the sole criteria of judgement are taken from within anthropology itself. If, instead, one were to accept that the majority out there, who are never going to be anthropologists anyway, might benefit from an injection of anthropological thinking and ethnographic facts, one might be more in favour of the idea of using a simpler language. In fact, some of the normally least readable anthropologists have shown this to be possible. Lévi-Strauss's *Myth and Meaning* (1978b) and his interview book with Didier Eribon, *De Près et de Loin* (1988), convey the main elements in his structuralism and his intellectual vision without losing, presumably, a single potential reader on the way. Many of us have something to learn from Lévi-Strauss in this regard.

The Post-colonial Critiques and the Loss of the Native. The post-colonial critique of Eurocentrism and the hegemony of Western forms of discourse is seen by some anthropologists as a confirmation that they were right all along. After all, anthropologists were always aware that knowledge was positioned culturally and geographically, and that local knowledges, although they differ from one another, can be equally valid. However, many post-colonial critics targeted anthropologists in particular (Deloria, 1969, may have been the first) for their tendency to describe traditional peoples as exotic and 'radically other'. The shift in power of definition urged by post-colonial writers and political movements seemed to imply that since the task of anthropology had consisted in identifying others, and since those 'others' were now perfectly capable of identifying themselves, anthropologists had basically lost their vocation. This view was met with a great deal of sympathy among anthropologists, who – unlike other scholars – perfectly well understood what was at stake, given their professional background. Now that the erstwhile natives had, in many cases, developed their own stories about their culture and their own views of relevant knowledge, anthropologists were seemingly left with the task of identifying and analysing native theories about culture rather than native culture. Or they could shift to the study of modern societies in the north. Both developments took place, increasingly so from the late 1970s, while at the same time many continued to study traditional societies, though it would now have to be traditional societies in transition.

In all likelihood, the loss of the native was a more serious blow to the identity of anthropology than most have been willing to admit. It is repeated over and over, like a mantra, that what distinguishes anthropology is its ethnographic method, not its subject matter (which would have been non-industrial societies in the past); but in practice, this implies that whereas the boundaries of the subject remain intact, its symbolic markers of identity have become problematic. For others produce ethnography as well, and anthropologists have discovered the significance of other sources of data, such as archives and mass media. The loss of the native was to anthropology what the loss of socialist Eastern Europe was to Western socialism. One had at the very most believed in it half-heartedly, but the moment it was gone, one discovered that an important element in one's self-identity was gone.

The post-colonial critique of the definitional power of the West thus undermined the anthropological confidence in two ways: it tainted the genealogy of the subject, turning anthropologists into the inheritors of a colonial science. It also told anthropologists that their work on 'the other' was irrelevant, unnecessary and probably harmful. Unfair as most of these claims might have been, they have led to a new soft-spokenness, a fear of offending the sensibilities of others, which can be quite paralysing.

More generally, it could be said that after the post-colonial critique of Western representations, the collapse of classic cultural relativism and the damaging postmodernist autocritique of the 1980s, anthropology has become modest in its claims, introverted in its intellectual perspective and even more reluctant than before to raise the Big Issues in generally intelligible ways. Other disciplines have emerged almost unscathed from these critiques, and so the historians, biologists and evolutionary psychologists, the media scholars and cultural sociologists have moved on to and occupied turf that might have been claimed by anthropology.

The complex relationship between anthropology and colonialism has been addressed time and again. Jack Goody (1995) has argued against the view that anthropologists in the classic modern period were closely allied with the colonial service, showing that the relationship tended to be strained and that funding often came from American foundations. Yet to the extent that members of the general public have any notion of what anthropologists do, they tend to identify the subject with Victorian explorers of some kind. The cliché of the anthropologist as a bearded explorer in a safari suit, a collector of bizarre exotica and a romantic soul ill-adapted to life in the modern world, is no longer being nurtured within the discipline, but in the outside world's occasional glances at it, it predominates (Shore 1996, Peterson 1991). The social or cultural anthropologist, whenever he (or, more rarely, she) appears in a popular film or novel, is more often than not a comical figure (see also Firth 1984). As Shore puts it (1996: 4), the academic anthropologist usually comes across as a pitiful character: 'useless knowledge, large ego, dangerously incompetent, but good as a figure of fun'. In spite of continuous efforts to tell people out there what anthropologists really do, the subject has been unable to get properly rid of its reputation for exoticism and its notion of 'the primitive'.

Aware of this reputation, anthropologists sometimes lose themselves in epistemo-logical hypochondria, and when they don't, at least they make sure that their isolation from the rest of society is not broken.

Serious and often well executed attempts to inform the outside world what we *really* do, somehow fail to reach the target group. There is an excellent website edited by Robert Borofsky, and an accompanying book series called Public Anthropology, but perusing it occasionally for pleasure, I honestly fail to see how it could attract anyone but other anthropologists or people with special regional interests. *Anthropology Today* has already been mentioned (see Benthall 2002b for a representative collection of 'greatest hits'); another recent example is Jeremy MacClancy's edited volume *Exotic No More: Anthropology on the Frontline* (MacClancy 2002), an almost breathtaking collection of articles representing the diversity of concerns in contemporary anthropology, from the organ trade in Brazil to tourism and hunger in Africa. Some years earlier, Ahmed and Shore's important book *The Future of Anthropology* (Ahmed and Shore 1995) similarly argued that anthropology should be essential for anyone's endeavour to understand the world, but I fear it was not widely read outside the subject, despite the epilogue by Anthony Giddens.

Di Leonardo (1998) has shown how other academics perpetuate a myth about anthropology being an exoticist, irredeemably romantic discipline unable to deal with the cultural impurities and symbolic power differences of the integral contemporary world. Criticizing Edward Said's denunciations of anthropology as a colonial discipline, she describes them as the result of a 'synecdochic fallacy, identifying the entire field either with past, clearly colonial work or with recent postmodernist texts' (di Leonardo 1998: 47). Mainstream anthropology, in fact, ceased to exoticize years ago, but the outside world has yet to discover it.

Loss of Confidence as Science. Everybody knows, even disregarding the sexist language, that today it would be academic suicide to publish a book entitled

'Anthropology: The Science of Man' or anything similar. The term 'science' does not feel right any more, when applied to what anthropologists do. In the mid-1990s, at the first of the annual debates organized by the Group for Debates in Anthropological Theory at the University of Manchester, the motion to be discussed and eventually voted over was 'Anthropology is a generalizing science or it is nothing' (Ingold 1996). It was rejected by 37 to 26 votes (8 abstentions). It is especially in the USA, however, that some of the most incendiary controversies of the last decades have centred on the concept of 'science', sometimes positing a contrast between scientific and postmodern anthropology, sometimes between scientific and humanist anthropology. All this leads us to recall the late Eric Wolf's much quoted statement to the effect that anthropology is the most humanist of the sciences and the most scientific of the humanities, but the truce, synthesis or compromise that Wolf suggests (and which his work is living evidence of) is all but absent in much of the contemporary debate.

The two most famous recent controversies which addressed the scientific potentials of anthropology were the debates over Derek Freeman's reinterpretation of Margaret Mead's Samoan research (Hellman 1996, Robin 2004) and the 'Darkness in El Dorado' scandal (Robin 2004). Both have been extensively covered and have reached the attention of readers well beyond the academy, so there is no need to reiterate the details. Briefly, then, Freeman (1983) argued that Mead's (1928) rosy view of Samoan adolescence was tainted by wishful thinking and poor ethnography. However, he was in turn criticized by other experts of the region (and a host of others) for simplistic biological and psychodynamic explanations. To outsiders as well as insiders, it might seem that Freeman's 'more scientific anthropology', which purported to show that Samoans were psychologically volatile and prone to violence, was just as one-sided as Mead's rather more idyllic picture. What seeped through to the general public from the controversy is likely to have been that anthropologists are unable to agree on even the simplest fact – in a word, that the discipline is in a mess.

The other controversy, which first erupted through a flurry of e-mails sent to anthropologists across the world in late 2000, concerned the investigative journalist Patrick Tierney's book about the Yanomami (Tierney 2000), which contained some extremely damaging criticism of an American research group's behaviour among this Amazon people from the 1960s onwards. The anthropologist who was part of the group, Napoleon Chagnon, was accused of various forms of misconduct, ranging from manipulating his evidence of widespread violence among the Yanomami to upsetting social cohesion by instigating conflict. It was eventually proved that the most serious accusation, namely that the research team had deliberately spread measles in a eugenic experiment worthy of Josef Mengele, was false. Some of the other accusations, however, appeared to be accurate. Chagnon and his defenders, among them many prominent sociobiologists, argued that the criticism was a part of a plot against the scientific approaches in anthropology that Chagnon advocated.

A believer in objective science and Darwinian explanations of cultural behaviour, Chagnon felt victimized by what he saw as the postmodernist, relativist mainstream of cultural anthropology.

Dust settled, the Tierney–Chagnon controversy revealed a discipline severely divided and deeply troubled in its self-identity as a science. As Robin (2004: 164) observes, no middle ground could be found between believers in quantitative methods and falsification of hypotheses, and humanist interpreters. The result was a stalemate, ultimately most damaging to the reputation of anthropology and the confidence of its practitioners, giving the impression that different schools of anthropologists truly lived in different cultural worlds unconnected by bridging principles of translation (see Borofsky, 2005, for the full story).

On a less dramatic note, anthropology has, on both sides of the Atlantic, quietly diversified into a jungle of theoretical perspectives with no dominant 'school' proper to be seen anywhere. It is the fruitition of what Edwin Ardener prophetically spoke of as 'the end of modernism' in anthropology twenty years ago (Ardener 1985). In this kind of situation, anthropology has become its own worst enemy when it comes to communicating with the wider public. Anthropology, torn and fragmented, has lost its professional confidence as the Science of Man. When anthropology occasionally makes it to the front page these days, what is on display is, disconcertingly, its dirty laundry.

Anthropology as a Subversive kind of Activity. No single explanation can account for the failure of anthropology to sustain a clear, visible, constructive public presence. Elitism, myopic specialization and the resulting relativism, cultivating complexity for its own sake, internal conflicts and loss of scientific confidence partly illuminate the problem. But what if we suppose the messages from anthropologists are often perfectly intelligible, well executed and nicely crafted, yet they still fail to arouse enthusiasm and interest among the reading public? One should not rule out the possibility that anthropologists are often understood, but disagreed with. Since anthropology 'makes the exotic familiar and the familiar exotic', to use Kirsten Hastrup's words, its perspectives continuously threaten to subvert values and ideas held dear by its potential non-academic audience. The very idea of anthropology as a cultural (auto)critique, defended by many of those who see the potential of a public anthropology, presupposes that there is a great demand for cultural self-criticism out there. This, plainly, may not be the case.

Some anthropologists may respond to this situation by offering humorous and light-hearted satires, 'Nacirema-style', about their own society. Eschewing a more messian role as solemn cultural critics, they may nevertheless contribute in a small way to an enhanced level of reflexivity. However, such a relegation of anthropology to a harmless trickster position in society smacks of defeat. As a colleague once remarked: Whenever an economist makes a statement, non-academic listeners may describe his message as 'interesting' or even 'important'. But when an anthropologist says something, the reaction is likely to be that it is 'fascinating'. Good, clean fun, in other words, but ultimately unimportant.

Comparing the present situation of American anthropologists to that of Margaret Mead, di Leonardo (2001) argues that the changed ideological climate has cast anthropologists in a new public role, which most of them are unwilling to take on. Mead thrived before the rise of the New Right, before the recent triumphs of a refurbished sociobiology, before the tangles of identity politics made it virtually impossible to generalize about 'cultures', 'before the global rightward tilt and recent neo-liberal triumph, before the corporate consolidation and increasing tabloidization of the media' (di Leonardo 2001). In the new setting, she intimates, anthropologists are welcome to exoticize their own culture in historical, entertaining and preferably cute ways, or to make wide-ranging pronouncements on human universals. Rejecting this discursive frame, anthropologists become invisible instead, keeping their subversive views to themselves and leaving the public arena to people burdened with fewer reservations.

Alternatively, they jump on the bandwagon and find a place in the public sphere by telling amusing anecdotes about how we are 'really' like New Guinea tribesmen. Di Leonardo notes, acerbically, that '[t]he attribution of "our" characteristics to "them", and vice versa, is always good for a laugh in popular culture' (di Leonardo 1998: 57). Although she is correct to point out the dangers of trivialization, one cannot help asking what is wrong with a laugh. In rituals of rebellion, from Max Gluckman's Zulus to Dario Fo's theatre (here we go...), laughter can both be an easy way out of a contradiction and an expression of serious social criticism.

Privileging Analysis over Narrative. This final argument is possibly the most important one. The partial explanations above give historical background and some sociological explanation of the failure of anthropology to communicate in the public sphere, but to my mind the single most important characteristic of anthropological writing is that it tends to be chiefly analytical. This means that it is more difficult to get into and less easy to remember than narratives. Stories are the stuff of life; analysis is for specialists.

When I carried out fieldwork in Trinidad, one of my most important collaborators was a regular contributor to the public discourse in Trinidadian society. He was a journalist and writer, he had a university degree from Jamaica and had written book chapters, but he retained an ambivalent attitude towards academic research, largely because he felt that its insistence on analysis 'dried out the river'. We often had a beer on the terrace outside his house in the evenings, and I might ask him a question such as: 'What exactly could be the consequences for a rural African girl if she marries an Indian man?' Instead of giving the folk model and its deviations, which he might have been capable of, he would almost invariably begin his response by saying: 'Let me tell you a story...' – often talking for fifteen minutes or more before allowing me to try to pull the analytic implications out of the story. If he gave a public talk, his notes barely filled the back of a supermarket receipt. Since his talks would consist of interwoven stories, he only needed a few keywords to remind himself of which ones to tell and in which order.

In contemporary anthropology, pleas for narrative have almost become a cliché. Our journals regularly bring theoretical discussions about the centrality of narrative, about narrative as a key to understanding life, about the ways in which the great narratives of history mirror the small narratives of personal lives, and so on; but we rarely get on with actually telling stories. Maybe this is a general professional affliction. Anthropologists are world champions at studying and analysing rituals, but many (most?) of us find it excruciatingly difficult to organize, or even take part in, rituals ourselves.

As always, there are exceptions here too. Katy Gardner's acclaimed stories from Bangladesh (Gardner 1997), which use narrative strategies derived from literature, have already been mentioned. A few years later, Gardner would encounter commercial success as a novelist with *Losing Gemma* (Gardner 2002), a psychological thriller set in India. Actually there are many brilliant narratives in anthropological literature, but they are usually hidden in analysis, making them inedible for general readers.

If we consider the successful interventions made by anthropologists in the past, whatever their differences they have one thing in common, namely a narrative thread and a clearly stated theme. Even *Tristes Tropiques* (Lévi-Strauss 1978a), that labyrinth of a book, has a theme crisply stated in the very first sentence: the author hates travelling and travellers, yet he writes a 500-page book about his own travels – how on earth is he going to do it, and what does he intend to tell us?

Anthropologists tend to resist simplicity, and often for good reasons. Reading the blurb on the cover of anthropological monographs, I usually conclude that it will in all likelihood be necessary to read the whole book in order to get the point. The time-consuming, slowly cumulative fieldwork process is in this way transposed faithfully to writing. The monograph has its twists and turns, its lacunae and adagios, just like fieldwork itself. There is a beauty in this. But there is also a problem. Phrased uncharitably, it is possible to say that the genre of written anthropology combines the worst of two academic traditions. The language game of the natural sciences favours lucidity and analytical clarity, a parsimonious style and a logically consistent argument. In mid-twentieth-century anthropology, this would have been the norm, certainly in Britain. The language game typical of the humanities, especially history, favours richness and complexity, eschewing simple solutions and easy ways out. This ideal has been predominant in late twentieth-century anthropology.

At the same time, many of the academics who favour 'richness and complexity' also tell stories, thereby bringing them closer to the worlds of non-academics. A model is provided by the historians. History is almost alone among academic subjects to fuse original research and popular writing in the very same texts. Outstanding historians like Simon Schama or Eric Hobsbawm, Emmanuel LeRoy Ladurie or Fernand Braudel are able to attract the sustained interest of very large readerships, while simultaneously producing new knowledge and fresh perspectives. Their books are based on narrative, usually chronologically linear, and are scrupulous in their attention to detail. Although he is a card-carrying Marxist, it is difficult to accuse Hobsbawm of being a reductionist.

The other kind of popular academic writer, the natural scientist, tends to choose a different strategy (although there is a clear overlap with the narrative structures of history in evolutionary theory). The essentially analytic argument in influential science writers like Steve Jones (1997) or Steven Pinker (2002) is punctuated with anecdotes, literary quotations, and stories from the contemporary media or from everyday life, thereby bringing life to what might otherwise have been a very dry riverbed indeed.

In the anthropological literature, there is a tendency to combine a penchant for complexity with a lack of engaging, sustained narrative – in the latter regard, it resembles natural science more than history. As a result, it appears that anthropological texts are readable only by other anthropologists, who have learnt – the hard way – to read them. When books of crisp, clear and entertaining writing are published, such as most of MacClancy's *Exotic No More* or Benthall's *The Best of Anthropology Today*, they fail to arouse attention outside the discipline itself: other potential readers, who may have skimmed through a few volumes of anthropology before, think they know what to expect and move on to the more exciting bookshelves of media studies, history or evolutionary psychology.

The Anthropologist as Public Intellectual

Jonathan Benthall, who has spent decades helping anthropologists to write intelligibly and well as the Director of the Royal Anthropological Institute and editor of *RAIN*, later *Anthropology Today*, muses that 'theoretically, anthropology ought perhaps to be the queen of the social sciences' (Benthall 2002a: 10). He then adds, immediately, that it should probably be seen as a 'service discipline' instead; small, but with the potential to influence 'more mainstream discipines'. But could it not be precisely its slightly countercultural character, which enables it to look at the world with fresh eyes from unexpected angles, that has the potential of placing anthropology in a central location? The myths of uniqueness that defined twentieth-century anthropology were very helpful in internal identity politics, but they created strong and impenetrable outward boundaries. If anthropology continues to surround itself with a mystical aura internally, the trade-off will consist in it being undersold externally.

The anthropologist as public intellectual, a 'professional stranger', is not 'the anthropologist as hero'. It is somebody who breaks with bourgeois etiquette by making the implicit explicit. In the introduction to his study of Creole elite identity in Sierra Leone, Abner Cohen (1981) makes some interesting remarks about what it was that defined a 'gentleman' in Victorian England. It was a set of subtle, implicit skills tucked away in the gentleman's bodily habitus. Like the trickster of many folktales, the public anthropologist unpacks and displays such embodied, implicit, apparently trivial snippets of social life, revealing them to be repositories of symbolic power. Quite often, the person who points out that the emperor is indeed naked, ought to be an anthropologist.

This book chiefly focuses on interventions through writing. A good case could be made for anthropological radio, film and television, but the mainstay of our intellectual culture has always been, and remains, writing. Now, there are linguists, folklorists and biologists who write syndicated columns in quality newspapers. Why not anthropologists? Quite a few of Benthall's own editorials in *Anthropology Today* might have been adapted to fit such a context. And, as Peterson (1991) points out, if anthropologists cannot represent themselves, they will be represented by others. He has looked at US tabloid stories featuring anthropologists, and has come up with stories such as the one featuring 'anthropologist Fritz Greder from Switzerland', according to which cannibals recently ate six aliens from space. An unsettling point made by Peterson is that during a random month, no stories featuring cultural anthropologists were printed in five of the leading quality newspapers in the USA, but eleven stories appeared in a similar sample of tabloids.

There are several ways of getting the message across. Popularization is one; ambitious overviews and even presentations of new ideas in sparkling prose are another; while intellectual interventions aimed at raising the public consciousness about some topical issue are a third.

The popularizer and the public intellectual are not always a single person – in fact, they can be opposed to each other. In order to be popular, the popularizer has to pander to widespread sentiments; she has to be an organic intellectual of sorts, sometimes stating the obvious, sometimes giving an apt and accurate phrasing of notions already held semi-consciously by the readership. She must convince the readers that she is on their side. The intellectual, according to Said (1993), Furedi (2004) and others, is obliged *to say unpopular things in a striking way*. The very point of criticism, in Foucault's view (2001), is to speak against the 'people', against received wisdoms and representations that are dominant. In making this argument, Foucault draws on the Greek notion of *parrhesia*, which refers to the activity of speaking against power in a way that entails a certain personal risk (Neumann 2004).

In spite of the apparent, and often real, contradiction between the role of the popularizer and that of the intellectual, many seem to combine the roles rather well. They do this by making statements which are perceived as outrageously provocative by parts of the target group, while confirming the pre-existing world-view of others. Richard Dawkins typically does this. His often rash, but pithy, attacks on any form of belief that does not conform to scientific rationalism are hailed as pure genius (or common sense) by people who have been in agreement with him all along, and are perceived as irritating or dangerous by various others. Margaret Mead's work had a similar function.

What makes Foucault's distinction ultimately unhelpful in our era is the difficulty in identifying hegemonies or dominant modes of thought. Is global capitalism, or neo-liberalism, hegemonic? This is claimed so often, routinely, that it rings untrue. At the level of economic practice, it may be the case; but among the chattering classes, it would have been something of a sensation if a respected thinking man or woman were to come out in defence of the World Bank and the transnationals. Or take multiculturalism in any of its guises. The idea that cultural variation within a society is OK and that North Atlantic societies ought to be able to accommodate immigrants without assimilating them is, perhaps, perceived as a daring and brave position by those who defend it. Moreover, at the level of political practice, anything smacking of multiculturalism is controversial in many countries – but among columnists, academics, writers and others who raise their voices in the left-liberal public sphere, it is more risky to defend the supremacy of Western culture than to advocate a greater sensitivity to say, the ancient wisdom of the East or South Asian family values. Mavericks like Slavoj Zizek (2000) or, closer to home, the anthropologist Jonathan Friedman (1997), who question the basic assumptions of multiculturalism, admittedly come across as braver and less predictable than the rest of us.

The sociologist Frank Furedi (2004), using Zygmunt Bauman's terminology, argues that while intellectuals were legislators in the past, they are now mere interpreters. Lacking the global vision and imperial ambitions of Jean-Paul Sartre, Furedi argues, contemporary intellectuals tell stories in a minor key and tend to limit themselves to specific interventions. They are institutionalized in the universities, fragmented through professional specialization, and complacent in their secure careers. The ongoing formalization of the recognition of skills through never-ending evaluations of research, auditing and other forms of 'Professionalization' (cf. Furedi 2004: 154) threatens to take the creativity out of academic life, and also contributes to isolating it further from society. Since the latter half of the twentieth century, we have witnessed a phenomenal growth in the number of highly educated people. While I was serving as editor of a bi-monthly cultural journal, I often wondered why its circulation did not skyrocket in the 1970s and in the 1990s, following growth periods in the system of higher education. The main reason may be that students are no longer encouraged to be intellectuals, but to specialize and become professionals, rather than waste their time on reading essays about this, that and the other.

Yet the situation is far from catastrophic. Anthropology has a pivotal role to play, and there exists something we might call the intellectual public sphere, where it can play its role. The view, common among cultural pessimists, that the public intellectual is disappearing because of McDonaldization, the closed circuits of academe, government instrumentalism or the predominance of mindless entertainment in the mass media may be partly true, but it is not particularly helpful. Besides, I suspect that it is not true. There are still a great number of highly specialized academics who are willing to go out of their way to intervene in matters of public importance, and both Great Britain and the USA have their share if one cares to look. But hardly any of them are anthropologists. That is the strange fact we are grappling with in this book. When people like Richard Dawkins describe religion as 'harmless nonsense', adding after 9/11 that he is now inclined to drop the word 'harmless', one must be forgiven for thinking that there ought to be a market for other kinds of intellectual.

Patrick Wilken (1994), in a thought-provoking pamphlet about anthropologists and the Gulf War, finds support from intellectuals such as Russell Jacoby, Régis Debray and Terry Eagleton when he concludes that the 'institutionalization of intellectuals [in routine university work] has severely curtailed their independence, made obsolete the role of the free-ranging generalist and signalled the rise of the professional specialist' (Wilken 1994: 9). This observation does not, obviously, concern anthropologists exclusively, but we should be especially receptive to the argument, given our dismal record in public intellectual life over the last half-century.

More anthropologists ought to function as intellectuals, addressing issues of general public interest in their habitual contrarian, unexpected and provocative ways. Although the demise of the public intellectual is proclaimed regularly, nothing in fact seems to be further from the truth. In the last decades of the twentieth century, the number of media – both kinds and titles – grew enormously. Although it may be difficult to be heard under such circumstances, due to the sheer noise and volume of simultaneous attempts of mass communication, nobody, and certainly no university academic, can claim that there is nowhere to publish. The democratized media situation offers something for everybody. Although it may ultimately lead to a general state of 'enlightened confusion' (Castells 1996) in large parts of the population, we should see the liberating potential in the fact that the time of the mimeo is long gone for the earnest academic.

An intellectual is a person who refuses to mind his own business. Unlike specialists, intellectuals are generalists; unlike the believer in pure, unadulterated knowledge, intellectuals have opinions. Unlike most members of the public, however, they also have considerable knowledge drawn from a variety of sources, and this can both make them influential and worth listening to. The true intellectuals, as Said (1993) said in his famous Reith lectures, thrive when they 'are driven by metaphysical passion and disinterested perceptions of justice and truth to denounce disingenuity and immorality, to defend the weak, to oppose imperfect or oppressive authorities' (Said 1993: 21). Anthropologists have a legitimate role to play as public intellectuals, and although I have given several explanations of why this has not come about, it still remains something of a mystery that so few take it on. This is because anthropology is so uniquely suited for public interventions, not least in the realm of politics. The emphasis on the local experiences, the alternative interpretations, the *Verfremdung* effect on our own societies and the not inconsiderable (dare I say it?) entertainment value of the stories we are able to tell, make anthropology a perfect launchpad for anyone wanting to engage the wider public in discussion about pressing or existential issues.

Like all intellectuals, our job partly consists in being speed bumps in the information society, by making easy answers to complex questions slightly more difficult to defend. We have a duty to remind the greater public that there is a world out there where knowledge is being produced slowly. Populism, in other words, is not the answer. As Einstein is reputed to have said: Make things as simple as possible. But not simpler!

What, then, does anthropology have to offer? There are obviously some topics which are best left to journalists and creative writers, although there is a fascinating grey zone between anthropology and those genres, just as the zone of ambiguity between biography and fiction has been debated extensively (in mainstream media, incidentally) in recent years. Like the members of any profession, anthropologists and their academic cross-cousins and other collaterals are best advised to concentrate on whatever it is that they do best.

Like many university-employed anthropologists, I have occasionally read MA dissertations wondering whether they contain any insight which could not have been included in a long, well researched reportage or feature article in a quality newspaper. Disturbingly, the answer is sometimes negative. Of course, an academic treatise should provide understandings that could not be obtained and digested during a week or so of clever journalistic research. Conversely, if engagement in the public sphere, frustrating and exasperating as it can sometimes be, is to be worthwhile, anthropologists have to offer something which is not already there. The question is, therefore, what are the unique insights that anthropologists can bring to the public sphere? Let me mention four kinds of contribution for now.

First, the comparative perspective and its accompanying *Verfremdung* or defamiliarization effects belong properly to anthropology. The insight that society could have been very different, that you and I could have held other values and had other expectations of life, is one of anthropology's greatest gifts to humanity.

Secondly, the anthropological insistence on the primacy of the insider's view, the lived experience of 'ordinary people' and the texture of their life-worlds, is usually missing even in the better newspaper articles about far-flung places. Again, this perspective can make a difference. As some of the examples in later chapters show, media impact often depends on the ability to convey gripping stories about individuals.

Thirdly, anthropologists are rather skilled at exposing oversimplifications by insisting on a more nuanced and complex view, be it in the realm of military expansion or that of biological determinism.

Fourthly, anthropologists (and academics in general) should be less afraid of stating the obvious (or that which, at any rate, is obvious to them). Whenever we move out of the ivory tower, the intended audience does not include people who can tell post-development from post-structuralism. Or who give a damn about the difference even if they know it.

–3–

Complexity and Context

A good article, I was once told, is shaped like a fox, with a pointed muzzle, some stuff in the middle, and an extravagant tail ending in an impressive flourish. This was the view once defended, tongue in cheek, by the distinguished geologist Thomas Weibye Barth, according to his son Fredrik.

Advanced students who plan their first venture into the field, or who have just embarked on a largish, library-based project, are normally asked by their supervisors about their research question. What exactly is it that they want to find out, and why do they bother? Most supervisors regularly encounter research proposals which are well executed at the level of theory, methodology and regional knowledge, but which lack something essential: a problem, an issue, a burning question to be explored if not necessarily answered, or an existential concern. These proposals are summarily returned to the fledgling recruit, who more often than not returns with one or perhaps a few questions. If the student has not quite grasped what scientific knowledge aims to do with the world, the proposal may contain too many questions, which is in practice tantamount to none. Unless corrected, the student will as a result write a disorganized and ultimately aimless text, possibly resorting to the lame excuse that the complexity of the material defied simplification.

In one of Borges's philosophical short stories, the ruler of a remote kingdom orders his cartographers to make him a totally accurate map of the country. After a number of false starts and rejections, they come up with a map which, when rolled out, covers the country completely – a map on a 1:1 scale. In other words, the world is there for us to simplify it. Naturally there are many alternative modes of simplification, and all the learned debates about epistemology, methodology and the ideological embeddedness of knowledge concern which simplifications, if any, are the most fruitful or defensible.

When you write an ethnography, you essentially carve a bit of the world into a plot with a narrative thread and/or heuristic value for formal modelling. If you are a writer of a positivist bent, you may use the empirical stuff to test a hypothesis; no matter what your persuasion in matters of methodology, you will presumably try to illuminate one or a few interrelated questions. Unless it is made clear what the issues at hand are, the reader may justly ask what is the point of the entire exercise.

It is sometimes said that what militates against a public anthropology is its inherent complexity. The public, the argument goes, wants simplicity – simple answers to complex questions, but what anthropology has to offer is merely more complexity. And so anthropologists may jokingly say, in a gesture of mock self-depreciation, that at least we raise the public consciousness to a higher level of confusion.

This will not do. There are impressive degrees of complexity in, say, Simon Schama's or Eric Hobsbawm's historical narratives, yet they succeed in attracting the sustained attention of thousands of readers. Popular science writing can also be very complex. The examples and arguments of Richard Dawkins's best books, such as *The Blind Watchmaker* (Dawkins 1986), can be followed by any diligent reader, but not even his enemies have claimed that these books lack complexity (even if his answers are, at the end of the day, always natural selection). The problem with a great deal of anthropology in this regard is dual: first, the writing isn't good enough to attract a non-professional readership. Second, it is not always made clear what the research questions are. Often, the anthropologist plunges into a complex intellectual territory without returning to the surface in order to show the findings to the reader. Uncharitably said, anthropologists sometimes give the impression of either holding the answer back or offering answers for which there are no questions.

The problem is not complexity as such, but a dithering attitude and somewhat coquettish refusal to be lucid and unequivocal. As a rule, in a debating contest, the most lucid contender is likely to win, even if his more oblique adversary has the best arguments. In an article about the assumed 'Islamophobia' of post-9/11 Britain, the non-anthropologist Kenan Malik concludes with a summary dismissal of multiculturalism:

> Diversity is important, not in itself, but because it allows us to expand our horizons, to compare different values, beliefs and lifestyles, and make judgements upon them. In other words, it allows us to engage in political dialogue and debate that can help to create more universal values and beliefs, and a collective language of citizenship. But it is just such dialogue and debate, and the making of such judgements, that contemporary multi-culturalism attempts to suppress in the name of 'tolerance' and 'respect'. (Malik 2005)

Malik here identifies multiculturalism *tout court* with a refusal to discuss the intrinsic qualities of any self-professed culture, including its unintentional side-effects of moral constipation and fundamentalist certainties. His positing of multiculturalism and universal values as opposites may be reasonable in the context of his polemical essay, but it is ultimately simplistic, as the anthropologist Terence Turner showed more than a decade earlier in his famous (among anthropologists, that is) article on anthropology and multiculturalism (Turner 1993). Turner distinguishes between a *difference* multiculturalism and a *critical* multiculturalism. Only the former fits Malik's bill. Critical multiculturalism is in effect an extension of the Enlightenment language of rights and equality, and takes it as its aim to counter the Western monopoly of definitional power. Including Native American history in school curricula in the USA, for example, would be an expression of critical multiculturalism. Had he been armed with this kind of distinction, it would have been more difficult for Malik to denounce the people who complained that Muslims were not sufficiently respected in the public sphere.

However, Turner's article failed to make an impact outside anthropology. Although it is mostly lucid, it does contain a number of linguistic knots, for example in an important paragraph near the middle of the text, where the author formulates the bridge between anthropology and critical multiculturalism:

> [W]hen anthropologists contextualize their ideas about culture by focusing on the ways cultural constructs mediate the social processes and political struggles through which people produce themselves and resist and/or accommodate asymmetrical power relations, and when they combine the critical decentring of cultural representations with the decentring of their own theoretical perspectives on those representations, then they will not merely have a base from which to complain about being ignored by multiculturalists, but a basis for making constructive critical contributions to the critical multiculturalist programme for a democratic culture. (Turner 1993: 422–423)

This means, roughly: anthropologists offer finely grained accounts of other people's cultures and the way their everyday struggles are being shaped by cultural ideas. However, anthropologists also critically question *their own* ideas and theories about how these cultural worlds come into being, since these ideas, too, are culturally constructed and have an ideological dimension. Anthropologists could thus tell multiculturalists that if they criticize their adversaries for providing a slanted and partial view of the world, by the very same token they have to question their own view of the world. If more people did this, society would become more democratic as a result.

The argument is far from trivial and could make a positive contribution to current controversies about multiculturalism, but in order to do so, it needs to be unpacked. The same point could be made about anthropological contributions to the ongoing debate about genetic engineering, which are far too important to remain tucked away in the inner circle of initiates.

Rather than looking at our own failures, however, it might be worthwhile to look at the successes of others. In the world of popularized science, which often contains a none too concealed political agenda, anthropology has been utterly marginalized for a generation or more. It is unlikely that the full explanation is the irreducible complexity of anthropological writings. Yet it may seem that the attraction of many of the most popular science writers consists in their ability to offer lucid, simple answers to seemingly enormously complicated questions; to cut the Gordian knot of contemporary confusion and provide crystal clear and easily understandable scientific reasoning in its stead. Anthropologists ought to take this situation very seriously indeed. Should not the comparison of cultures, questions of human nature, the diffusion of ideas and the rise and fall of civilizations be the domain proper of anthropology? Well, these problem areas certainly haven't been part of mainstream anthropology for some time, and others have filled the void. Just consider the following for a start.

The Large Canvas

A few years before the turn of the millennium, a book listed under 'anthropology' appeared in bookshops worldwide, and through many paperback printings, it steadily became a great success for its author, turning him into a science writer of the first order. The book, written not by an anthropologist but by a physiologist, evolutionary biologist and science popularizer, claims in its subtitle to tell 'a short history of everyone for the last 13,000 years'. Jared Diamond's *Guns, Germs and Steel* (Diamond 1997) is a hugely ambitious cultural history which, to an anthropologist, smacks of Harris and perhaps some of White's more accessible work. It is a charming, enlightening and entertaining book, which belongs firmly to the riddle genre rather than the just-so story. The initial question, raised for Diamond by a New Guinean, is, simply, 'Why is it that you white people developed so much cargo [goods] and brought it to New Guinea, but we black people had little cargo of our own?' (Diamond 1997: 14). Well, Diamond says, this book is an answer to that question. Combining evolutionary theory, ecology and demography, Diamond argues powerfully and often persuasively that things are not what they seem, very much in the way a non-Marxist materialist anthropologist might have done a generation ago. Coincidences, population movement and ecological circumstances explain, in Diamond's book, why human groups developed in such different ways. Although the account is sometimes simplistic, the overall picture adds insight and fulfils its mission as a powerful argument against racism. In short, all my tribal affinities tell me that it is a shame that the book wasn't written by a social or cultural anthropologist. In Diamond's view, human nature is constant; what varies are ecological factors.

A few years later, Diamond did it again, with *Collapse: How Societies Choose to Fail or Succeed* (Diamond 2005). This is another fact-rich book, flattering to the general reader because it is easy to read, and its argument is more complex than that of *Guns, Germs and Steel*. In *Collapse*, Diamond relinquishes purely materialistic accounts and includes social and political factors as well (thus the verb 'choose' in the subtitle). The book, a cross-cultural, historical as well as contemporary survey of a kind that went out of fashion in anthropology many years ago, has an obvious message to its readers: many civilizations were at the peak of their glory and achievement, seemingly invincible, immediately before their inevitable decline and fall into oblivion. So how do our societies measure up? Diamond's answer is that we collectively have to make some difficult decisions, the sooner the better.

In the realm of large-scale cultural history, anthropologists do occasionally still try to provide global overviews. Eric Wolf's magnificent *Europe and the People Without History* (1982) exemplifies an approach that is more historical and less naturalist than Diamond's, but which can still be seen as complementary to it. In this book, Wolf also parades the unique contribution anthropology has to make, insisting on seeing world history from non-European viewpoints. Peter Worsley's *The Three Worlds* (1984), a more sociological variant, is more contemporary and less historical again, but it shares a potentially wide appeal and interdisciplinarity with the other books mentioned. Keith Hart's (2000) book on money in an unequal world, moreover, is also a wide-ranging, non-specialized overview, and it was marketed as a general non-fiction ('trade') book. Others could also have been mentioned, even if it is true to state that the generalizing overview of cultural history and the contemporary world is rare in contemporary anthropology, and it is scarcely encouraged by the guild. Is this because such overviews inevitably become superficial and unsatisfactory at the level of local detail? Maybe, but if that is the case, then anthropology could do with a less puritan attitude.

Additionally, there is a far too weak an engagement with the general intellectual debate about human nature. Criticisms by anthropologists tend to be directed inwards, reaching people who don't need them since they already agree with the arguments. Let's face it: after nearly a century, Mead's Samoan work remains the most famous anthropological contribution to the debate about human nature. Always controversial within and outside anthropology, it was eventually confronted with an equally one-sided perspective – the publication of Derek Freeman's *Margaret Mead and Samoa* in 1983, five years after Mead's death. Freeman took great pains to show that Mead had got most of her facts wrong and was totally mistaken about the nature of Samoan society. In fact, he claimed, violence, rape and suicide were common occurrences. However, Mead's book was not quite as simple as it has been represented retrospectively, by Freeman and others. In a lengthy appendix called 'Samoan culture as it is today', Mead says the following, among other things:

> But it is only fair to point out that Samoan culture, before white influence, was less flexible and dealt less kindly with the individual aberrant. Aboriginal Samoa was harder on the girl sex delinquent than is present-day Samoa. And the reader must not mistake the conditions which have been described for the aboriginal ones, nor for typical primitive ones. Present-day Samoan civilization is simply the result of the fortuitous and on the whole fortunate impetus of a complex, intrusive culture upon a simpler and most hospitable indigenous one. (Mead 1977 [1928]: 216)

Be this as it may, the attraction of Mead's numerous popular books lay in their insistence on the open-ended and flexible character of human nature. She drew striking contrasts between 'personality types' and cultures, persuading thousands of adoring readers of the almost limitless permutability of the human mind. Now, a Margaret Mead of our time would have difficulties in being taken seriously (cf. di Leonardo 1998, 2001). Contemporary intellectual debate about human nature has its epicentre very far indeed from Mead's world of early conditioning and mindboggling cultural variation. As most readers will have noticed, the biological sciences have achieved a presence in the public sphere in the early twenty-first century which is markedly different from the situation only a couple of decades ago. And nowhere is the rise to public prominence of biology more striking than in public coverage of matters relating to human nature, an area which was for a long time dominated by theologians, philosophers, literary people and social scientists.

A few years ago, the influential editor and literary agent John Brockman (1995) expressed the new confidence among natural science enthusiasts by launching the term 'the third culture', intended to cover the invasion of natural scientists (mostly biologists) into the traditional domain of the humanities. This was justified, Brockman argued, by the fact that the big issues of human existence had been forgotten in the humanities, where thousands of fine minds were keeping themselves busy by squaring the circle or splitting hairs. The vacant slot was destined to be filled by clever natural scientists who offered more exciting theories about human nature than their scholastic, introverted colleagues across the university square. Brockman's programmatic statement formed the gist of his introduction to a collection of interviews with prominent natural scientists talking about their ideas about humanity.

This development has come as a surprise to many onlookers, including not a few academics. Just as many people around 1980 assumed that Thatcherism and Reagan-omics were simply temporary aberrations not worthy of serious attention, a majority of intellectuals at the same time believed that understandings of humanity based on biology would never again be dominant after the demolition of a certain kind of biology gone mad in 1945. Among humanists, E. O. Wilson and Richard Dawkins were perceived, one might say, as the Reagan and Thatcher of the human sciences.

Well, they were wrong. Neo-liberalism remains the dominant ideology today (if anything, it is more omnipresent than ever), and biological accounts of human nature are spreading like ... an unusually fit genome: neo-Darwinist templates of thought enter into psychology, economics, religious theory and not least folk notions of what it entails to be human. The largest research project of the final years of the twentieth century was the Human Genome Project (which retrospectively appears as a mountain that gave birth to a mouse), and popular science books about the biological foundations of anything you might care to think of (as well as a couple of things few of us care to think of) become airport bestsellers. These books are well written, lively and sparkling with wit and confidence, and they make standard academic books appear tired and dull. This makes them relevant for the quest of this book. How on earth are they doing it?

Human Nature and Kinds of Complexity

For years it was difficult to take the spokesmen (nearly all of them *were* men) of biological accounts of culture seriously. Their obsession with territorial instincts, sex and violence led to an obvious neglect of phenomena such as language, art and technology, a fact which inspired the geneticist Steve Jones (1997) to quip that the theory of natural selection can tell us everything about phenomena such as opera or sex – except, of course, the interesting things.

The situation in the early twenty-first century is different. The new generation of writers, who call themselves evolutionary psychologists rather than sociobiologists, concentrate on understanding the working of the mind. While their predecessors tended to see language on a par with grunts and grooming among chimpanzees, and saw egotism in all interaction, current evolutionists have come to terms with the uniqueness of verbal language and altruism, and some of them readily admit that the genes do not always know what's good for them (e.g. Kohn 1999).

One of the brightest stars in the sparkling space of evolutionary social science has in recent years been Steven Pinker of the MIT, who published a large book called *The Blank Slate: The Modern Denial of Human Nature* in 2002. As the title reveals, the book develops an innatist alternative to the presumedly widespread idea that humans can learn anything because their mind is, *pace* Locke, a blank slate. When it was released, the book was highly praised by reviewers, especially in the USA; the reception in Europe was more mixed. The British science journalist Matt Ridley nevertheless says in his blurb testimonial that this 'is the best book on human nature that I or anyone else *will ever read*' (emphasis added). Quite apart from revealing an enviable knowledge of the future, this kind of statement suggests that we are witness to the birth throes of a religious movement. That, if nothing else, is reason good enough to dip into the revealed truth offered in Pinker's work as a science popularizer.

Pinker is a more sophisticated theorist than many of his kindred spirits; I enjoyed his intelligent and enlightening book *The Language Instinct*, and began this book in anticipation of an attempt to develop a true synthesis. Alas, the book turned out to exemplify all the typical weaknesses of this kind of literature. This must be seen as an opportunity lost, since Pinker, a neuropsychologist specializing in the study of language, could have placed himself in a position enabling him to bridge gaps rather than deepen them. The book reveals variable and often poor knowledge of what social and cultural scientists actually do, and it is based on a silly premise, namely the idea that the main characteristics of the human mind must be either inborn or acquired (as every non-specialist knows, they are both, simultaneously). The depiction of his opponents' views comes close to parody, and Pinker's own position is consequently more rigid than his arguments suggest, and more wide-ranging than his facts allow.

The central argument is that the human mind has evolved through natural selection, which is interpreted narrowly, here as in many other neo-Darwinist accounts, as individual competition for offspring and genetic fitness. Pinker also wishes to show that a wide range of human activities are ultimately biologically based and can be traced back to the struggle for survival in the 'environment of evolutionary adaptation' (EEA). There are lots of deep issues to be grappled with here, not least concerning the relationship between group, individual and ecosystem in the dynamics of evolution. Ecologically literate anthropologists like Bateson (1978) and Ingold (2000) – unsurprisingly absent from Pinker's account of the social sciences – have written intelligently and authoritatively about these issues.

Another crucial question concerns the relationship between biology, culture and freedom. Pinker is right in pointing out that social scientists have not generally taken it sufficiently seriously. The only problem is that he himself does not look at the complex interactions between individual and group, individual and sub-individual entities (genes, cells etc.), or biology, culture and individuality. He offers the simplest conceivable answers to some of the world's most difficult questions.

The paucity of nuance is astonishing. For example, Pinker argues that parents and other environmental factors have no important effects on the personality of a child. This position is as absurd as its opposite, behaviourism (the doctrine claiming that environmental factors account for everything, inborn characteristics for nothing). For there cannot be many who seriously believe that it makes little difference to the personality of a child if it grows up in Somalia or Iceland, in the inner-city ghetto or in the middle-class suburb?

Pinker is ungenerous, sometimes bordering on the disingenuous, when he makes it his business to depict the arguments of his opponents. This is most obvious when he cursorily and with reference to few if any sources writes off 'the left' for its pathetic habitual thinking (for example regarding gender roles), but he is not much more credible when he deals with academic research. In one place he mentions a few famous social thinkers who have allegedly refused to accept the innate aspects of the human mind (from Plato to Lévi-Strauss), obviously unaware that Lévi-Strauss, for one, has spent his long and productive life documenting the innate structures of the mind.

Writers of the this kind usually come into difficulties when they embark on the topic of free will. This is as true of Pinker as it was of Dawkins and indeed Darwin himself. If one correctly identifies the complex relationship between inheritance, the social and natural environment and freedom, then the doctrine about the genetic programmes of the mind becomes a watered-down and relative kind of truth, of little direct use in formulating slogans and policies. Pinker resists this temptation. Yet he admits that if he does not like what the genes ask him to do, he will ask them to 'go and jump in the lake'. But if he and everybody else possesses this kind of freedom, what remains of the evolutionary origins of the mind? Quite a bit, to be sure. But not much more than Emile Durkheim, Clifford Geertz and other social constructivist *Prügelknaben* have conceded time and again: we are born with innate predispositions, but they always articulate with the environment, with coincidences of circumstances and with the exertion of choice, leading to an almost incredible variation between cultures and between individuals.

There are many logical weaknesses and undocumented, but no less brashly presented assumptions in Pinker's book. This makes it all the more surprising that the book was met with almost unanimous applause in the American media. This is not because he says something new. The main selling point of this kind of book is that it offers simple answers in a world which is generally overflowing with ambiguity and confusing complexity. The answers 'seem right' in the same way as popular horoscopes: they are persuasive until one thinks about it. That this model of humanity can also easily be used to justify neo-liberalism (see Matt Ridley's excellent *The Origins of Virtue*, 1996, for an explicit connection) is also not exactly a disadvantage in today's market.

This kind of map is unable to account for the complexity of the territory. There is more 'both and' than 'either or' in the world. The biological contribution to our understanding of ourselves is necessary and important. Presented as a monologue, however, it sounds like one hand clapping.

Although I have serious misgivings about Pinker's style of argument, one cannot help but admire his achievement. His book is based on a mass of research, and he succeeds in making the reader approach a seemingly worn-out problem – the nature–nurture issue – with renewed curiosity. I think it is Pinker's skills as a writer, his ability to turn tedious research into good stories, and not his ultimately simplistic conclusions, that explain his success. In other words, as this book made it, densely packed as it is with references to scientific analyses, then there are readers out there for other ambitious, complex accounts as well.

So Where are the Anthropologists?

Although it is easy to dismiss Pinker's attack on social science in *The Blank Slate* as an overblown war on straw men, anthropologists and other humanists have no reason to remain smug and self-satisfied when they are faced with questions concerning human nature. It is true that both humanities and social sciences have shied away from the big questions about human existence, especially those involving large-scale cultural history (of the Diamond kind) and human nature (of the Darwinian kind). It can in fact be argued that many of us offer intelligent and elaborate answers to questions nobody has asked. If pressed, I suspect that most of us would prefer being near the question rather than being offered a mass of irrelevant answers. The evolutionists are right on target in this regard. They deserve better than being met with indifferent hostility.

Changes may be imminent, at least in Europe. The American situation appears to be hopelessly politicized and polarized, attacks and counterattacks having been depressingly predictable since the publication of Edward O. Wilson's *Sociobiology* in 1975. According to Chris Knight and his collaborators (1999), social and biological anthropologists in Britain had not really spoken to each other between the Royal Society conference about ritualization among humans and animals in 1965 and a similar, but smaller conference on ritual and the origins of culture in

1994. A few years later, a number of social anthropologists contributed to a volume about 'memetics' (Aunger 2002) dominated by Darwinian scholars, and later still, a symposium organized by Harvey Whitehouse (2001) brought together different views on the role of evolution in shaping religious beliefs and practices. Perhaps social anthropology is keen to find its feet again after postmodernism, and maybe mainstream anthropology is beginning to probe for ambitious and robust modes of explanation which can be reconciled with their proverbial, and laudable, attention to local detail. Certainly, the new evolutionary psychology seems more relevant and is better informed about cultural variation than the old sociobiology of the 1960s and 1970s, whose macho obsession with sex and violence, and manic search for adaptive functions everywhere in cultural practices, could hardly win the sustained attention of many sociocultural anthropologists. Many of the positions taken by the sociobiologists were so embarrassing that they were usually passed over in silence – except, for example, when someone like Ingold (1986) pointed out, with exasperation, that E. O. Wilson (1978), happily oblivious of intellectual history, had reinvented E. B. Tylor's comparative method from the late nineteenth century in his energetic attempt to 'reintegrate' the social sciences into biology.

The re-branded Darwinist social science of the 1990s and 2000s, evolutionary psychology, really does appear to have moved away from the crude reductionism represented in the previous generation. Usually drawing on proper knowledge of social science and cultural variation, it does not presuppose that culture is per se adaptive in a biological sense (which would have been an absurd position anyway), but is instead concerned with identifying evolved cognitive mechanisms that developed in response to selective pressure and which remain part of our cognitive architecture today, although they no longer necessarily serve an adaptive function. Evolutionary psychologists are interested in things like religion and reciprocity, they develop theories about the first strike in prehistory and the role of gossip in early language, and it may seem as if the conditions for fruitful interaction across the intradisciplinary divide have been greatly improved over the past couple of decades.

Evolutionary psychology tries to solve what we might call Wallace's problem. Hailed as the greatest biologist of the nineteenth century by Gregory Bateson, Alfred Russel Wallace, who developed the theory of natural selection independently of Darwin, believed that the human body was clearly a product of natural selection (which he, incidentally, saw more as a systemic or ecological process than one based on individual competition), whereas the immense complexity of the human mind needed another explanation, since he found it difficult to believe that primitive peoples needed a mind enabling them to build cathedrals or compose Beethoven's Ninth Symphony, which they were never going to do anyway. Darwin responded to Wallace's challenge in *The Descent of Man*, by stating that primitive man would need as much intelligence, inventiveness and ingenuity as he could possibly get in order to survive, in other words that the staggering complexity of the human mind was a result of natural selection, just as much as he (women, of course, were not yet seen as independent agents in the mid-nineteenth century) needed his opposable thumbs and bipedal gait. The central issue engaging evolutionary psychologists, and which should also engage social anthropologists, concerns – provided Darwin is right against Wallace – what exactly this evolved mind looks like: to what extent it gives instructions that still guide our thought and behaviour, and, conversely, to what extent it is flexible and open-ended.

However, apart from a small handful of attempts, the dialogue remains all but absent. The controversy surrounding Patrick Tierney's *Darkness in El Dorado* in the USA in 2000, briefly discussed in the last chapter, brought out bitterness, rage and supremacist rhetoric on both sides in the United States. There was no middle ground available at the time.

In Europe, including the UK, it would be an overstatement, to put it mildly, to claim that evolutionary biology has become a trendy subject in social anthropology. In fact, the relationship is largely one-sided: evolutionary psychologists publish provocative tracts denouncing the *naiveté* of unreformed and unconverted social anthropologists and similar social scientists, who rarely bother to respond in kind, or even to rectify facts and correct misunderstandings.

Social anthropologists typically react to the challenge from evolutionary psychology in four ways: (i) Darwinists are irrelevant even if they may be right (that is, their truths are trivial or marginal); (ii) Darwinists are relevant, but have a fundamentally misguided notion of what it is to be human; (iii) Darwinists are relevant and sometimes right; or (iv) Darwinist social scientists and other social scientists play different language games – they ask qualitatively different kinds of question, and as a result, their theories are incommensurable and do not talk to each other. All these views are widespread among social anthropologists, the third view perhaps less so than the others. Many seem content to observe that human biology places certain constraints on our potential for thought and action, but add that what needs attention is the variation which exists within these boundaries. Others argue that the objectivism and naturalism proposed by Darwinians need to be countered by approaches emphasizing systemic complexity, dynamic process and individual agency. Yet others (but I suspect a small minority) try to sift the material and arguments offered by the Darwinists in search of nuggets of gold.

Seen from a humanist or social science perspective, there are many serious problems with most neo-Darwinist accounts of humanity. The architect and cultural commentator Charles Jencks (2001) relates a story from a lecture by Edward O. Wilson, where the famous sociobiologist claimed, among other things, that humans had a universal, inherited abhorrence of snakes (Jencks's daughter had just smuggled one into the country), that the hourglass figure was the objective ideal of female beauty (what about Twiggy, and what about the plump mother goddesses of neolithic Europe?), that humans had an inherited preference for art featuring flat landscapes with neatly trimmed grass, water ponds and clumps of trees (i.e. suburban America, or an Ivy League university campus) and so on. Pinker, incidentally, shares Wilson's views of aesthetics – people are ostensibly inclined to prefer paintings featuring grass and water, and he mentions, as one of three causes of art, 'the aesthetic pleasure of experiencing adaptive objects and environments' (Pinker 2002: 405). They both come close to the now thoroughly discredited sociobiological view that culture can be explained through its adaptive functions. Most contempory evolutionary psychologists accept, at least at a programmatic level, evidence to the contrary: culture can be exceptionally unadaptive in Darwinist terms.

There has been substantial criticism of simplistic adaptationist arguments from within the natural sciences. Among the most influential critics are Richard Lewontin and the late Stephen Jay Gould in the USA, and Steven Rose in the UK; but the geneticist Steve Jones, by no means a militant critic of biological explanations, also remarks, on the assumed heredity of alcoholism, that it appears to be hereditary in Britain but not in Iran (Jones 1997). In the same book, *In the Blood*, a companion volume to the eponymous BBC series, Jones also mentions that although it can be argued that homicide somehow relates to inherited aggression, it is a much more interesting fact that murder frequencies vary hugely between big American cities and big British cities, and that this cannot be understood without taking into account the differing numbers of handguns in the two countries.

Neo-Darwinist accounts of human nature tend to be one-sided and unsatisfactory. But as the philosopher Imre Lakatos never tired of pointing out, purely negative criticism never killed a research programme. In other words, we need more convincing alternatives. In the academic literature of anthropology, several such alternatives exist, from Gregory Bateson's system ecology to Tim Ingold's ecological phenomenology, but these impressive research programmes so far remain to be translated into a form, and a language, that communicates beyond the group of initiates.

The kind of complexity needed for an account of human nature to be palatable for anthropologists has been described often enough. A typical example, though not very well known in the Anglophone world, is Edgar Morin's description of sacrifice (Morin 2001). A staple in anthropological research, and a topic which has also occasionally attracted the attention of evolutionists, sacrifice can be accounted for in many ways. There are Darwinian, structural-functionalist and culturalist narratives about sacrifice. Morin, however, distinguishes between no less than seven levels of signification in his account: (i) It is a response to anxiety or uncertainty, alleviated through offerings to the Gods; (ii) It signifies obedience to stern demands from the same Gods; (iii) It signifies reciprocity at the symbolic level towards other groups; (iv) It is a magical exploitation of the regenerative force of death; (v) It transfers evil to a victim being subjected to exorcism; (vi) It represents a controlled channelling of violence, and finally, (vii) It reinforces the solidarity of the community (Morin 2001: 38). None of these levels can be reduced to another without losing something essential on the way.

In other words, the complexity of human activities is many times greater than assumed in simple causal accounts. This is not to say that such accounts are necessarily simply wrong, nor that they cannot be useful, but only that if we want to understand a phenomenon, a general account (be it Darwinian or otherwise) is at best a beginning. The questions are being raised inside and outside of academia, and anthropologists are well positioned to put themselves in their vicinity.

A Small Handful of Anthropological Contributions

Whatever one's feelings about the new Darwinism, here is a game that anthropologists and other social scientists cannot afford not to play. And, as the examples of Diamond and Pinker show, the reading public is far from unable to absorb academic complexity, provided it is wrapped in good writing and presented through a straightforward, credible argument. There are lamentably few contemporary anthropology books which are interdisciplinary, address a general intellectual audience and take on the big issues of human nature/culture. But there are some. Michael Carrithers published, some years ago, a book with the tantalizing title *Why Humans have Cultures* (Carrithers 1992), subtitled 'Explaining Anthropology and Social Diversity'. Carrithers's aim is to reconcile the perspectives from social anthropology with those of Darwinism, no less. He identifies sociality as an inherited, evolved trait of humanity, and builds his account of human lives from this starting point. The book is excellent, written in a lively style with engaging examples – and yet, I suspect that few of you have read it. His main message to the Darwinians seems to be: 'Yes, you are right, but it is more complicated than that.' Like Brian Morris's *Anthropology of the Self* (Morris 1994), it engages with evolutionary theory but notices the shortcomings of its most simplistic versions, and as a result, what it has to offer in the end is complexity. This is honourable and intellectually defensible, but it is not by itself going to solve our problem. At a certain point, one must have the nerve to allow one's complex vision to come together in a clear, brief, pithy statement.

Let me mention a couple of other examples. An almost unknown book is Peter J. Wilson's *Man – The Promising Primate* (Wilson 1980), which, like *Why Humans have Cultures*, is an ambitious attempt to bridge the gap between evolutionary and culturalist accounts. Wilson, whose *Crab Antics* (1978) is a modern classic of Caribbean studies, here argues that 'the evolutionary characteristic of the primate order is a tendency towards increasing generalization of morphology' (Wilson 1980: 151). Put differently, the flexibility and lack of fixity typical of humans are products of evolution. Although the argument is not entirely original, the material utilized by Wilson, primate evolution and the peculiarities of the branch that became humanity, deserves attention. Yet he failed to get it.

Similarly, Adam Kuper's book about culture and human evolution, *The Chosen Primate* (Kuper 1994) is possibly his least cited book. Kuper's account, beginning briskly with the unforgettable sentence 'We are all Darwinists now', presumably startling half of the readership at the outset, moves on to a carefully argued, and cautiously ambivalent, account of the debates about human evolution and culture.

The book has a clearly phrased problem, namely what human evolution can tell us about culture. Kuper then embarks on an entertaining and enlightening story, which interweaves the history of human evolution itself with the history of research and controversy on the topic. It is also a very witty book peppered, like his *Anthropology and Anthropologists* (Kuper 1996), with anecdotes and amusing asides. Finally, it is a nuanced book, written in the spirit of dialogue, and though the author ultimately concludes that biology can tell us precious little about human society, he makes important concessions to the 'hard science' of evolutionary biology on the way.

Why did this book fail to make it? For one thing, it does not seem to be a favourite among anthropologists, who may have regarded such fraternization with the enemy as unwarranted frivolity. However, it could be argued that the main target group is not other anthropologists, but interested lay people – the same people who would later buy and read Pinker's *Blank Slate*.

It is difficult to blame the lack of success on complexity in this case (and the other anthropological books mentioned). Kuper is an elegant writer, lucid and witty, and easy to follow for an educated reader. Depressing as it may seem, a main reason for the book's confinement to limited circles could be that potential readers understand its message, but either disagree or are uninterested. Following an equivocal discussion of gender roles, culture and biology, Kuper concludes:

> Some writers have suggested that there are universally acknowledged, bedrock values; but it is hard to find any ethical principles that command assent in all cultural traditions. Others might prefer to seek ... an ethic based on our real human nature, but it is hard to be sure what ingredients make up that common, underlying nature, and even if they could be identified they might be worth modifying if we can do so. (Kuper 1994: 207)

This is an entirely sensible and intelligible view, presented in crisp prose, which follows logically from the material presented in the chapter – and of course it is not exactly headline fodder. It is unlikely to reinforce the readers of *The Economist* in their conviction that humans are competitive and individualistic, nor will it comfort readers who see complexity as an obstacle with an elegant, simple explanation.

All three books under review share a common trait: ambivalence. In this they differ from the brasher, more confident, shiny-armour-clad Darwinian stories which promise powerful, compact answers to questions of staggering complexity. This quality of some current popular biology makes it reminiscent of religion. But it also catches the attention of the intelligent layperson who wants the world to make sense. Still, the question of human nature is far too important to be left to believers in simple genetic explanations. As Brian Morris pointed out in a memorable passage in *Anthropology of the Self*: Creating a human being can be compared to baking a cake. You need a recipe for sure (DNA), but you also need ingredients (soma; nourishment), an oven (the environment) and a cook (subjectivity or will). Only if you are able to see all four elements simultaneously will you have understood what it takes to bake a cake. This is the message that needs to be conveyed in ways that catch the attention of the general public.

The point is not, obviously, that Darwinism is wrong, but that the 'state of nature' is a fiction. As Kuper showed in his historical account of the idea of primitive society (Kuper 1988), the fiction has persisted among academics up to the present, even if it has repeatedly been shown to be false. As Barnard (1999) has shown, Bushmen and Aborigines have a widely differing symbolic culture in spite of a similar level of technological development and comparable group complexity. And as Ingold points out (2000), it is only through ontogenesis – continuous engagement with the environment, social and natural – that innate properties can develop at all. So the environment, natural and cultural, matters quite a bit no matter how one sees the matter. Again, as Geertz says, the only way to be human is by way of culture – there is no substratum underneath that messy, ever-changing conglomerate of cultural and social conditioning, inborn characteristics, individual whim, environmental circumstances and pure coincidence. The point is that these perspectives can and should be popularized, even if recent attempts have been, often undeservedly, unsuccessful.

Memetics and the Anthropologists

If regular evolutionary biology can be written off – if unwisely – as irrelevant to the enterprise of modern sociocultural anthropology, the same can definitely not be said of its 'culturological' offshoot, memetics. First developed as an afterthought to *The Selfish Gene* (Dawkins 1976), the terms 'meme' and 'memetics' have spread phenomenally (its adherents sometimes point out, lamely, that the notion of the meme has been an extremely successful meme). Dawkins's original argument was that genes are a kind of replicator (they are programmed to produce copies of themselves), but that other kinds of replicators might exist, for example in culture. An idea, a ditty, a skill such as origami, might thus be seen as gene equivalents, competing for survival and propagation in the spaces of cultural stuff. Dawkins has scarcely developed the idea of the meme himself, but others have, including the philosopher Daniel Dennett (1995), the psychologist Susan Blackmore (1999) and the physical anthropologist Robert Aunger (2000, 2002). As the meme has apparently proved such a successful exemplification of the theory of memetics, it is curious that none of its defenders seem to have referred to the original coinage of memetics, in Richard Semon's 1908 book *Die Mneme als Erhaltendes Prinzip in Wechsel des Organizchen Geschehens* [The Mneme as Conserving Principle in the Exchanges of Organic Processes]. Semon's concept of memes is related to Dawkins's usage, but it did not catch on.

In spite of appearances, memetics is not a branch of biology. Unlike sociobiology and its affiliates, it is not an attempt to expand the scope of biological explanations in order to be able to subsume human thought, behaviour and culture under the Darwinian umbrella. In fact it is qualitatively different from the materialism often encountered in evolutionary psychology and other branches of sociobiology. It is a *metaphoric* Darwinism, and the commonalities between human sociobiology and memetics could be summed up in two points:

- The Darwinian principles of evolution are relevant in more contexts than commonly assumed, notably with reference to human life.
- There exists only one form of scientific knowledge, and ultimately all phenomena can be accounted for according to the same procedures of discovery.

In spite of a shared commitment to unitary science and Darwinian thought, the differences between sociobiology and memetics are also obvious, if not always spoken about. Sociobiology, including evolutionary psychology, teaches that human behaviour should, if possible, be interpreted in the light of long-term evolutionary strategies, in other words that humans should primarily be seen as mammals who respond to selective pressures in the same ways as other mammals would. Memetics is a different kind of intellectual endeavour, and it should be noted that Dawkins initially proposed the concept in order to modify the extreme claims he had made in his creative development of Hamilton's Rule, where, among other things, he describes organisms as mere survival machines for the genes. The meme, he says, is a different kind of replicator from the gene, and although it spreads according to the same general mechanisms of selection and competition, the memetic domain is autonomous and has no direct link to genetic survival. Daniel Dennett's 'universal Darwinism' elaborates on Dawkins's original sketch and proclaims that the Darwinian principles of natural selection are a 'universal acid' that render other attempts at explanation redundant in most if not all domains.

The contradictions between sociobiology and memetics have not been properly worked out in the literature, and authors like Pinker want to have it both ways: Humans are primarily mammals responding to selective pressures in their reproductive strategies, documented in nurturing, parental investment, personality development and so on; and at the same time, ideas spread according to the same principles of selection, but quite independently from genetic selection. However, if ideas do evolve and spread autonomously, it is easy to see that they inevitably come into conflict with the postulated biological needs; there is no reason to assume that ideas and norms should be consistent with genetic strategies unless they are determined by them; and if they are determined by them, they do not constitute an autonomous, different kind of replicator. Some memeticists, such as Susan Blackmore, have noted this discrepancy, and her development of memetics in *The Meme Machine* (1999) may be the most consistent achievement so far.

In other words, memetics belongs to cultural studies and not to biology. It is a metaphorical Darwinism using natural selection in an analogous way, and as such it has no more in common with Darwinism proper than Durkheim's physiological metaphor for society has with physiology proper. Human thought cannot, according to memetics, be reduced to selective pressures operating at the level of the genome, but it can be explained in the same theoretical terms. The similarity is one of pattern resemblance, not of causation.

Consider E. O. Wilson's famous statement in *On Human Nature* (1978: 167): 'The genes hold culture on a leash. The leash is very long, but inevitably values will be constrained in accordance with their effects on the human gene pool.' This will not do for a memeticist (e.g. Dennett 1995: 470 *et passim*). Wilson's claim is too substantivist (he implies that genes determine values in the last instance) and thus not sufficiently formalist (according to memetics, natural selection can operate on any kind of replicator).

Seen from the perspective of cultural studies, the memeticists win hands down. It is all too obvious that many of the products of the human mind, including some of the enduring ones, are non-adaptive in an evolutionary sense. As Lévi-Strauss says somewhere: Stating that societies function is trivial, but stating that everything in a society is functional, is absurd. This kind of view is fine with the memeticists. They, or at least some of them (Dawkins, Dennett, Blackmore) nevertheless claim that memetics is not merely a loose analogy to genetics: meme evolution 'obeys the laws of natural selection quite exactly' (Dennett 1995: 345). The three principles of natural selection are variation, heredity and differential fitness among the replicators.

Anthropologists have noted, with some irritation, that none of the leading advocates of memetics discuss earlier work on cultural diffusion, which is very considerable. This is forgivable; the most original research is sometimes produced by newcomers to a field who are unburdened by conventional assumptions. However, ignorance of earlier research may also lead people into the same pitfalls as their predecessors.

Memetics is a kind of diffusionism: a research strategy which aims to discover how cultural ideas and practices spread from their point of origin outwards, and promises to explain why some cultural items become very widespread while others do not. The question raised is excellent. Alas, so far, memetics, at least in its popular form, has not delivered anything but pompous programmatic statements peppered with anecdotal evidence. What was a mitigating idea in Dawkins comes, in Blackmore's and Dennett's development of it, close to absurdity.

Nobody doubts that cultural diffusion takes place. Ideas and practices spread. Many are keen to understand why it is that some cultural ideas and practices travel fast while others do not. Why did Microsoft and Wintel computers conquer the world when the arguably superior products from competitors like Apple did not? Why do the fashion-conscious spend their savings on dressing in clothes that others deem horrible? Why does English spread faster than any other second language? More generally: to what extent are societies/cultures influenced by each other, and how should we go about improving our knowledge of the cultural dynamics involved?

Diffusionism was fashionable a hundred years ago, in competition with an evolutionism that owed less to Darwin than to social theorists like Marx and Spencer. Diffusionists generally regarded people as less inventive than was assumed by evolutionists, and did not believe in universal laws that permitted all societies to develop along the same lines. However, most diffusionists were also evolutionists: accounting for the diffusion of particular traits, they argued that the more advanced would normally replace the more primitive.

The problem of classic diffusionism, as anthropologists might tell the memetic-ists, is that it is difficult to show whether or not apparent similarities are due to diffusion, and more critically, that a single cultural item is never the same after having been moved from one context to another. This is partly because it is modified en route, and partly because the context is different in the new setting, leading its meaning and functioning to change.

Some eighty years ago, diffusionism was replaced by functionalism as the dominant theoretical approach in social anthropology. Functionalism advocated the detailed study of single societies and viewed them as self-sustaining entities upheld by the interaction of a number of institutions such as inheritance, kinship practices, division of labour, and religious beliefs and practices. Functionalism had its obvious flaws as a theoretical programme, but what it did offer was ethnographic description of the highest quality, revealing some of the complexities at work in actual existing societies. Memetics has, thus far, offered nothing of the kind.

Other objections to the fledgling theory of memetics have also been raised. What, for example, is the unit? Is it the first movement or just the first eight bars of Beethoven's Fifth Symphony? Blackmore and Dennett seem to think that memes could be identified in both memories, actions and artefacts; in other words, that memes exist both in brains, behaviour and things. Aunger (2002: 164) takes issue with this view, and argues that memes exist only in brains. Memes, in other words, are recipes. But seemingly identical results may be the result of different recipes (as the critique of diffusionism showed), so caution is recommended before wide-ranging conclusions are drawn.

A common objection to the metaphoric use of the gene-meme, is that unlike genes, ideas (or memes) are not copied perfectly. The 'fidelity' of the copying process is low, as any academic who has been quoted out of context, for example by a newspaper, knows.

A more major objection, as pointed out by the philosopher Mary Midgley (2001), is that ideas are not granular. Adam Kuper adds that culture traits are not the equivalent of philosophical notions (Kuper 2000: 181), and that it would be very misleading to pretend that they were. Maurice Bloch agrees with this view, pointing out that knowledge cannot be separated from its context of action (Bloch 2000). Dan Sperber (2000), criticizing memetics from within an evolutionist framework, argues that since the development of knowledge takes place within evolved domain-specific frames of disposition, ideas move through inferences, not mere copying.

Another serious question, since selfish-gene biology is the source of inspiration for the metaphor of the meme, concerns where the selective pressure comes from in the case of memetics. Regarding genetic selection, the answer is straightforward enough: survival and procreation. Concerning memetic selection, the answer is less obvious. Dawkins is applauded by Dennett when he says (1976: 214), uncharacteristically vacuously, that 'a cultural trait may have evolved in the way it has simply because it is *advantageous to itself*. This sounds like chance to me, and besides, what does it mean that something is advantageous to itself when the context is one of fierce competition? On the other hand, all memeticists to my knowledge happily use personal pronouns (most often 'we') when they describe the selection process – and yet, they reject the idea that an autonomous, discerning human subject exists!

In any serious theory of cultural transmission and diffusion, one expects presentation of empirical material. No such luxury is afforded us by the leading lights of memetics. At a general level, the theory repeats facts which have been familiar since the rise of sociocultural anthropology as an academic discipline in the 1870s: that humans transmit information through symbolic communication and are therefore different from other animals at least in this respect; that there is considerable, but imperfect vertical continuity in knowledge, skills and values when culture is transmitted between the generations, and that considerable borrowing across cultural boundaries takes place, often blurring the boundaries and leading to phenomena such as symbolic domination, hegemonies and hybridities. More recently, globalization research has looked into the consequences of the revolution in communication and information technology for cultural dynamics.

The examples marshalled by leading memeticists are few and weak. Dawkins mentions paper origami, Dennett the first four notes of Beethoven's Fifth Symphony. They seem to share a general fondness for ditties, fads and clearly delineated practices such as the ban on shaving among traditionalist male Sikhs. These examples are, as every anthropologist knows, meaningless without a consideration of their context. Why is it that certain simple pop tunes conquer the world, while more substantial contributions to music do not? Try to answer the question without considering context, and you see what I mean. These particular songs are likely to be reminiscent of tunes people have heard before, they are aggressively marketed on television, radio and through other media, they connect with other aspects of youth culture deemed desirable, and so on. The same could be said about blue jeans, except that a pair of Levi's lasts longer than most pop songs.

When the ageing Marcel Mauss wrote about swimming techniques in 1935, he noted that the way he was taught to swim in the late nineteenth century, filling his mouth with water and spitting it out 'like a small steamer' as a way of marking the rhythm of each stroke, was by now long obsolete. How can one account for this change? Presumably someone got the bright idea that filling one's mouth with seawater did not help locomotion. In memetic terms, such a change might be described as a copying error, but this is not a helpful term here. The new swimming technique is more efficient, but it is also easy to think about changes in cultural practices and ideas that reduce a particular form of efficiency in order to promote some other quality. Changes in the dominant swimming techniques must be seen in the wider context of other cultural changes – in gender relations, in attitudes to the body, and probably in the rise of industrial society and its values.

The spread of the *hijab* or headscarf among Muslim women worldwide from the late 1990s onwards could be another test case for memetics. How can that be explained? Lots of factors could be mentioned, including a growing ideological influence from conservative Arab forms of Islam such as Wahabism disseminated efficiently thanks to global means of communication and Saudi oil money; the increased muscle of the Arab world and subsequent pride in Muslim identity following the oil crisis of 1973–74; an identity formation centred on the Palestinian problem and US/Israeli imperialism; a post-colonial feeling of symbolic domination triggering counter-moves in the form of traditionalism ... it is difficult to see how the concept of the meme could help us understand this phenomenon better. Historical context is crucial here, but so is human reflexivity and emotions such as resentment, humiliation and self-esteem. Without a subject, or a collectivity of subjects, sifting, organizing and prioritizing between alternatives, no understanding is possible. As Bloch has remarked (2000: 198), 'the fact that the habit of making noodles came to Italy from China does not explain why Italians make noodles'.

The two major anthropological objections to memetics can be summarized as a chicken-and-egg problem and a problem of context. Firstly, where does the selective pressure come from in the case of memes? They compete for 'brain space' say the defenders of memetics – well, but who or what allocates 'brain space' and on which criteria? Secondly, nothing has a meaning by itself, and culture is not granular. For anything to spread, it must make sense in the new context and for that purpose it must often be transformed, consciously or not. If female circumcision is a meme, it can only be understood in relation to a large number of other memes and their mutual interactions; in a word, a full symbolic universe that renders the world meaningful to the people who inhabit it. Rather than sensitizing us to the complexity of symbolic meaning (a precondition for ideas to survive), memetics asks us to split up culture into basic components, which can nevertheless never be understood unless they are seen as parts of larger entities.

Memetics may be beyond salvation as a theoretical project. However, it raises a few questions which are just right for anthropology seen as an endeavour of public relevance. It sees human culture as part of nature yet rejects the simplifications of human sociobiology, and it asks highly pertinent questions about cultural transmission, cultural diffusion and cultural change. The notion of contagion is useful and has not been properly explored in cultural studies, including anthropology. But – I repeat – without an understanding of the human subject, no advance will be made, and of course, as any ecologist will agree, context is everything. Curiously, in attempts at applying memetics, the biology itself seems to suffer. In Ingold's words, the genotype exists 'in the mind of the biologist' (Ingold 2000: 382). The ambition of offering a simple and straightforward analytic account of the human mind has led to an untenable abstraction.

The lesson from the experiment of memetics is that we have to do better: those of us who feel that memetics is insufficient have to come up with a better alternative than merely stating that things are more complicated than this. Saying 'things are more complicated' is like having endless meetings to avoid making a controversial decision.

The anthropologist's account of human nature has to be holist – it must include the recipe, the ingredients, the oven and the cook – and it must supersede the conventional culture/nature divide. Looking in the direction of biology, it is likely to find more by way of inspiration in ecology than in genetics. It must also take human experience seriously as an area of enquiry. These general delineations notwithstanding, several paths are possible and might shed light on the human condition. The field is open: with a handful of exceptions, there have been few attempts since the Second World War to develop a theory of human nature which draws on biological knowledge without succumbing to the temptations of easy fixes.

But is it possible? In a speech given in Lund in 1820, the Swedish poet Esaias Tegnér famously said, possibly with Hegel in mind, that 'What is obscurely spoken is obscurely thought' (*Det dunkelt sagda är det dunkelt tänkta*). To this one must add that obscure thought may sometimes be necessary, but it is not virtuous in itself. Style tends to mirror content; as Sutton (1991) points out in his discussion of successful popularization in anthropology, his chosen writers' style of writing and presentation of argument are congruent with their message. Anthropologists therefore need not shy away from complexity in their popular writings, but should rather strive to find an authorial voice that carries the message of complexity beyond the guild. Anthropologists should stop fidgeting and get on with it.

Lucidity and Complexity

Gregory Bateson once advised scientists to set up placards at the limits of their knowledge, stating that the world is 'unexplored beyond this point'. Sound advice no doubt, but it seems that in the case of social and cultural anthropologists, these placards have been too numerous, while they tend to be far less common among biological anthropologists or at least their popularizers.

The main problem which has been identified in this chapter is that of simplification and generalization. There seems to be a great demand for simple answers to complex questions, and anthropologists refuse to offer them – however, that refusal doesn't exactly make the headlines, and it does little to change the world or to influence people's thoughts about the world. It may be difficult to be accessible without compromising one's commitment to complexity, but perfectly sound ways of dealing with the problem exist, as the best of the writing in popular science and history shows. For example, concentrating on one or two arguments at a time often helps. Being extremely specific, dealing with only one example and revealing it to be very different from what it might seem, is another method. Lucidity does not necessarily preclude complexity. No matter what one's strategy, it is quite clear that views of human nature are far too important to be left to neo-Darwinists to work out.

The issues discussed in this chapter are being debated in the elite media – the *TLS*, the *New York Review of Books* and so on. But they are also far from absent in mainstream media, and the voice of anthropologists might make a difference there too. In September 2004, the largest Norwegian daily, *VG* (circulation over 400,000), published a story featuring a well-known psychiatrist who had argued, at a professional meeting, that our evolutionary history had equipped humans with a propensity for unflinching loyalty towards close kin and an ever-weakening feeling of solidarity towards others. It was claimed in the article that the psychiatrist, Prof. Berthold Grünfeld, also suggested that this 'scientific fact' meant that ethnic conflict was unavoidable. I was then busy at work on an early version of this chapter, and realized that an opportunity to turn theory into practice was at hand, and so I submitted the following article, which was printed in the newspaper, slightly abbreviated, a few days later. The example hopefully suggests that even very modest and theoretically trivial work can sometimes be worthwhile.

The Predicament of Community

Is xenophobia natural? The question was recently raised following the claim by psychiatrist Berthold Grünfeld to the effect that people 'are made for living in small, territorially based groups'. Therefore, Grünfeld said, according to *VG*, 'strangers from other territories entail a threat [to the group's integrity]'.

Naturally, Grünfeld was met with criticism, initially from biology professor Inger Nordal and the minister of local administration, Erna Solberg. His point of view evidently appears unattractive in a culturally complex society. But suppose he still happens to be right? After all, it may seem as if people have in all times been suspicious of the neighbouring tribe, have attacked newcomers driving their cattle to the waterhole, have built fortresses and not least told nasty jokes about the people on the far side of the lake?

Grünfeld is right to some extent, but the idea that people are only able to feel solidarity in small groups is clearly wrong. How should one otherwise explain a phenomenon such as American patriotism?

All over the world, people live in groups based, to a greater or lesser extent, as common identity and mutual trust. The 'glue' keeping the groups together may be thick or thin; it can be easy or difficult to become a member of the group for those who come from the outside, and the groups vary in size. But all groups have something in common, and the most interesting shared feature in this discussion is that *not everyone can be a member*. In other words, they have boundaries. They deny people entry. Often, boundary-marking takes place through negative stereotypes, that is prejudices. This is far from being a Western or European speciality. For example, research has indicated that an important reason why Europeans for a long time held that cannibalism was widespread in Africa, was that *neighbouring peoples* had spread rumours about this or that group being cannibals.

People thus have a tendency to feel solidarity and trust towards 'their own' and to keep 'the others' at bay.

So far, we must concede that Grünfeld is right. But from here onwards, it becomes more complicated. A major part of human cultural history is the history telling us how groups have amalgamated, assimilated outsiders, split into smaller groups, shrunk and – especially – grown. This means that there is no simple answer to the question of who are 'one's own' and who are 'the others'.

It may be the case that some sociobiologists still believe that humans are ultimately adapted to living in small groups of hunters and gatherers, and that all later developments – from the agricultural revolution onwards – are unnatural and slightly undesirable. But even if we stick to hunters and gatherers as our example, the 'state of nature' according to some, it quickly becomes evident that not even that condition was particularly natural.

Archaeological findings from southern Africa suggest that in a certain period in our prehistory, tens of thousands of years ago, the human groups grew very rapidly, from a few dozen individuals to a hundred or more. An influential explanation of this change is that language appeared around this time. When people were able to discuss the weather, common acquaintances and recent events such as a successful hunting trip or the birth of a child, they were enabled to keep larger communities together.

This description is a simplification, but the point remains: humans have not known a 'state of nature'. We are naturally equipped with an ability to dream and fantasize, worship invisible gods or criticize those who do it, make plans and persuade each other, trust people or gossip about them. It we are going to bracket this aspect of life, in order to develop a simple and elegant explanation of human folly – well, in that case, the theory becomes so crude that it fails to explain anything at all.

During the last centuries, nations and modern states have emerged. They have been described as 'imagined communities' because anyone who pleads allegiance to a nation is forced to use his or her imagination to believe in their existence. We cannot see them. 'Norway' is an invisible entity. A society which is able to propagate and maintain the belief, trust and loyalty of millions towards something this abstract and huge, is worthy of respect. Nations are abstract and flimsy, yet many are not only willing to cheer for their athletes, but given the right kind of pressure, many are even willing to go to war on their behalf.

This was not always the situation. A couple of hundred years ago, most European armies consisted of professional soldiers and conscripted peasants.

National loyalty was minimal to non-existent. At that time, the local community would have been the most important focus of identification for most, though for the upper classes, the cosmopolitan, international community of aristocrats mattered the most – and the men and women of the church were, for their part, willing to sacrifice anything for the supranational religious community.

So who is going to claim that certain kinds of communities are 'more natural' than others?

It may be true, as some argue, that contemporary nations are troubled. Travelling, migration, the Internet and global popular culture contribute to a weakening of the sense of national community in many countries. Young people develop sympathies and commonalities across national borders. Immigrants often have two places they can call home, not just one. English has become the second language of the world. Many feel that they belong to several groups that are important to them. Perhaps they have a religion, a nationality, a local community, an education, a special interest, a sexual orientation or simply a personality that makes them feel at home in many kinds of communities, in their own country as well as abroad. Besides, there will always be a few who take an especial pleasure in breaking out of the groups and insisting that they are unique individuals, full stop.

If, in spite of all this, Grünfeld should still turn out to be right, one can at least feel relieved in one respect. For in that case, Muslim fundamentalism is impossible and clearly doesn't exist. Islam is a religion encompassing a billion individuals. Most of them will never meet; they look different and speak different languages. If it is true that we are genetically programmed to feel solidarity only with that intimate circle of people who live in the same place as we do, who we know personally or at least indirectly – well, in that case it is impossible to imagine anyone being willing to sacrifice everything for an abstract entity such as a religion.

The predicament nevertheless remains. All groups, no matter what they are based on, demarcate differences towards others. There is no final solution to this problem. The best alternative, provided what we desire is peace and cooperation, is to encourage many kinds of overlapping communities. Instead of regarding a country like Norway as a kind of extended family (of four and a half million), we might envision it as a mosaic where the inhabitants have something in common, but are also allowed to be different. In that case we shall have several points of entry into the imagined community, and the ticket cost will not be prohibitive for all those who do not imagine that they are descendants of Harold the Hairy [legendary ninth-century chieftain, described in official history books as 'the first king of Norway']. The good news is that the long cultural history of humanity shows us that this is possible. And it remains a question of will, not biology.

The intended readership of this article, one must be allowed to say without accusations of being patronising, was people who did not necessarily have more than a vague idea about anthropology, biology or science in general. *VG* is a right-leaning tabloid which rarely goes out of its way to defend immigrants, and which has often run campaigns against illegal migrants and 'asylum tourists'. The preferred afternoon newspaper of university-educated, left-of-centre Norwegians is the slightly more upmarket, and much more politically progressive, *Dagbladet*. I imagined the readership to consist of engaged citizens who might be inclined to believe, as many do, that when all is said and done, humans are driven by inherited biological instincts, and that 'we' are probably never going to approve of Muslims anyway. My ambition was to encourage them to think the issues over once more, to make their world slightly more complicated. The attempt may not have been successful: the article, printed in nearly half a million copies, did not elicit a single reaction that I know of, neither in print nor in my e-mail inbox. I include it here only in support of the argument that it is perfectly possible to argue against simplistic biological determinism without leaving the everyday lived reality and the everyday language of the average citizen, and that it is our duty to do it more often.

What kind of complexity is missing in this sample of journalism? First of all, it lacks empirical contextualization, making a number of grand, unsubstantiated statements and presenting its examples in a telegraphic form. This would not be acceptable in a book, no matter who the audience. Secondly, it does not work out the argument systematically, does not bring in difficult examples or good counter-arguments. In a longer essay or a book, the intellectual work exemplified here would rightly have been dismissed as shoddy and lazy. Yet (and here I gallantly rally to my own defence), the point of an article of this length is to encourage the readers to think along unfamiliar lines and to question ideas some of them may habitually take for granted. If it succeeds in adding a drop of complexity to the debate about xenophobia (which, I regret to admit, this article appears not to have done), then a text of this kind has succeeded.

–4–

Fast and Slow Media

Many conflicting demands are placed on scholars in the humanities and social sciences these days. Universities are being restructured, curricula and course plans standardized (in Europe, this is known as the 'Bologna process'). Staff are encouraged, sometimes forced, to apply for external funding for their research, often through extremely time-consuming application processes involving colleagues from many countries. The teacher–student ratio has gone up, the working day is fragmented by e-mails, meetings, admin work; universities are being redefined as a kind of business enterprise, there is increasing pressure on academics to be 'societally relevant', and on top of it, the population explosion in higher education has created a more competitive environment, forcing us all to publish more than before, in amongst the almost continuous mutual evaluation and the sprawling minutiae of contemporary university life. In smallish non-English-speaking countries, there is concern that publications should 'meet international standards', which is small-country newspeak for 'published in English abroad'. (Which means that publication in the *Botswana Journal of Social Constructivism* might count more than an article in a domestic journal with a rejection rate of 90 per cent.) But just as we need it more than ever before, the time which can be devoted to slow work is shrinking fast for most of us. Some may compare their situation, therapeutically, to that of Kafka, perhaps, who had a tedious office job during the day and wrote intense prose at night. Not that this kind of pretentious comparison ultimately helps.

Others opt out of mere academic work. Ron Robin, a professor of communication and history, has identified a new kind of intellectual, the 'hybrid scholar', who stays away from the industrial machinery of the new universities and instead writes popularized work based on other people's research (Robin 2004). Now this is a perfectly respectable niche to occupy as long as one remains within the bounds of common decency (Robin deals at length with various cases of plagiarism). However, his analysis of controversies in academia, which involve both anthropologists and historians, indicates that when these conflicts are allowed to enter the swirling world of the fast media, anything can happen. His conclusion is, in fact, that 'the medium indeed is the message' (Robin 2004: 25). He explains that 'the use of a particular medium dicates the terms of debate; it has a significant impact on the controversies' lifespan, their narrative structure, and their tone' (ibid.). Actually, he says, the use of mass media and virtual communication on the internet 'reflects fundamental changes in the status of professional gatekeepers, the rise of a new pluralism, and significant shifts in the geopolitics of academia' (ibid.). Many of his examples indicate that speed is indeed heat, as the physicists taught us long ago. The faster the medium, the more vitriolic and bombastic the debate. In cyberspace, he says, 'this type of instant pluralism sometimes increases dissonance and intensifies conflict' (Robin 2004: 24). It's plain common sense to state that speed encourages simplification. When the first trains appeared, Britons were concerned that they were psychologically harmful because their speed made it impossible to take in all the details of the passing surroundings. The same principle tends to apply in intellectual debate.

This presents a problem for anthropologists (and other academics) who wish to engage in the public sphere, since the form of presentation in which they specialize is unsuitable for the dominant regime of communication. Yet using this obvious fact as a pretext for remaining aloof from the mass media, on principle and for eternity, is hardly a satisfactory option for everybody.

A Hint of Doubt, a Drop of Complexity, a Subversive Remark...

One of the few metropolitan anthropologists who has a regular media presence is Micaela di Leonardo, who writes for *The Nation* and is occasionally contacted by mainstream media for comments on various current issues. So when does 'the fourth estate' contact di Leonardo? With audible exasperation, she lists some of the occasions when she has been rung up by journalists (di Leonardo 1998). One TV producer wanted her views on why some men are sexually attracted to very obese women. Another wanted her to take part in a Valentine's Day show on love and courtship ritual, and she has also been asked for her views on why 'symmetry' seems to arouse people sexually all over the world. Yet another journalist wanted a capsule anthropological analysis of why women were buying Wonderbras. (Not being a woman, I don't have a clue as to what Wonderbras are, and I don't think I'm going to find out.) She has also been asked for her thoughts on why, despite so many decades of feminism, American women still enlist the aids of hair dye, make-up, plastic surgery and diets, and doesn't this prove that they are genetically encoded to attract men to impregnate them and protect their offspring. Finally, a *Good Morning America* producer begged her to appear on a show with the theme 'Is Infidelity Genetic?' (1998: 354). What can one say? Kudos to di Leonardo for not dismissing the US public sphere after a series of such dismal episodes, but continuing to search for points of entry that might open up the magic of anthropology for a greater audience!

These examples reminds one of Johan Galtung's term 'pyjama sociology', coined after he had been contacted by a journalist who wanted the sociologist's explanation for the decline in pyjama use in the Western world (Galtung, personal communication). The trivialization of serious knowledge entailed in the examples is obvious, and in addition, all the examples mentioned by di Leonardo indicate the prevalence of a pop version of genetic reductionism, which is incidentally less widespread in Europe than in the USA. Not that it is entirely unknown on this side of the Atlantic either. The now retired anthropology professor Arne Martin Klausen once served on an expert panel in a popular science magaine in Norway, but he resigned after only a few months. The only questions he received, as a 'scientific expert in anthropology', were of the generic kind: 'Why do the Negroes (*sic*) have kinky hair?'

However, I must say that my own experience is different. Whenever I am contacted by the Scandinavian media for comments on current affairs, they typically ask for comments on social and cultural issues. During the last week, journalists have phoned or e-mailed me for comments on national differences in leadership styles, following an international survey which indicated that such differences might be consequential; on the cultural changes that took place in the 1980s following the worldwide political turn to the right; on the roots of contemporary Norwegian nationalism in nineteenth-century romanticism (this was an Italian journalist visiting); on the new, proposed university law which threatens to remove the last remnants of democratic governance in universities; on the images of Norway projected abroad by the Foreign Ministry (helped by Mark Leonard's Demos institute); and, finally, I was asked to review the Indian author Arundhati Roy's latest collection of critical interventions.

Sounds like heaven? Well, not quite. The agenda is set by the media, and our job largely consists in filling in a few details or offering a soundbite or two – or deciding not to, in which case they sooner or later find another academic who is willing to do so. Now, it would not be a self-serving or even defensible view that newspapers are evil incarnate. Granted that they are not peer-reviewed journals, anthropologists can still often contribute a drop of complexity, a hint of doubt or a subversive remark. Given that our existence depends on our licence to quote from others and indeed to describe their lives, we should not be above allowing others to quote us.

This ought not to be taken to imply that there should be no limits whatsoever. Anthropology can, for example, easily be reduced to a form of light entertainment by the media in what di Leonardo speaks of, disparagingly, as 'the anthropological gambit': 'The attribution of "our" characteristics to "them", and vice versa, is always good for a laugh in popular culture' (di Leonardo 1998: 57). This facile juxtaposition of 'us' and 'them', in her view, obliterates concrete power relations, context and tormented histories, and serves only to trivialize cultural differences. In this spirit, she attacks Lévi-Strauss's speech given at his admission in the Collège de France, where the revered master compares that ritual of admission with a similar ritual, involving symbolic power among a group of Canadian Indians. In di Leonardo's harsh words, this 'droll likening of a powerful, state-sponsored intelligentsia to a powerless group of North Americans is an example of chutzpah as obscenity' (1998: 66). I fail to see the obscenity and do not think, as a rule, that there is too much humour and laughter in the attempts by anthropologists to communicate to outsiders. Comparison can be stupid, superficial and misleading, but at the end of the day, even comparisons of a Gary Larson type can bring us slightly closer to each other. Audiences are not uncritical receptacles, and 'the anthropological gambit' can help them to laugh not just at the follies of their leaders but even, occasionally, at themselves. As a matter of professional ethics, the distinction between kicking upwards and downwards should be kept in mind.

A number of contrasts can be posited between academic research and journalism, making for an unruly and frustrating relationship. Foremost among these is the contrast pertaining to speed: academic work is slow, while journalism is fast. Associated with this is the contrast between complexity and simplification. Journalists typically present issues in everyday language, work under serious constraints regarding both time and length, and are usually expected to tell stories with a simple message.

In most societies, moreover, the craft of journalism is not highly regarded. In the rich countries, journalism is increasingly associated with the sensationalism and commercial bias of the large-circulation press. Surveys about the public's perception of the trustworthiness of those engaged in various professions indicate that in North Atlantic countries like Britain and Norway, journalists are to be found near the bottom, along with politicians.

Media frequently ask academics to contribute, to allow themselves to be interviewed and to furnish journalists with relevant facts. Many academics routinely refuse to cooperate with the media, given the very considerable differences in aims and methods between research and journalism. It can often be appropriate for academics to remain aloof from the media world. Their views are likely to be represented in simplistic ways by the journalists, and the kind of research they are committed to is often irrelevant to the media anyway. It nevertheless occasionally happens that the fields of interest between the two professions converge. In the case of social anthropology, this is increasingly the case in so far as growing numbers of anthropologists study contemporary modern societies, on topics where there is already considerable media interest, such as multi-ethnic society and migration, national cultures and cultural change, changing kinship structures, 'new work', tourism, consumption and so on.

As mentioned, anthropology does have a strong media presence in certain countries, where anthropologists regularly comment on current events, write newspaper articles, debate minority issues on television, write polemical books for general audiences, and so on. In this engagement, it is easy to see the predictable dilemmas: the academic qualities of the anthropologist's work are quickly forgotten, and only their opinions come across. The anthropologist's views appear in a context defined by considerations other than those that initially motivated the intervention, and the outcome may be frustrating to the academic, who feels betrayed and misunderstood.

On the other hand, several anthropologists have become highly skilled at using the media to influence public opinion, some of them functioning as public intellectuals with political agendas and the ability to explain them. The relationship between media and academics should thus not be seen as a form of one-way parasitism, but as a complex relationship where there is a struggle over the definition of the situation. Mainstream mass media may even have an untapped potential as vehicles for complex ideas.

A Note on Norwegian Exceptionalism

A bonus reward that comes from engagement with the public sphere is the possibility that one's own shortcomings and weaknesses are illuminated by relevant criticism from unexpected quarters. There is real danger in exposing oneself in this way, but if anthropology is going to influence the dominant patterns of thought in the anthropologist's own society, there is no other way.

As indicated, the public sphere in Norway is unusual in that anthropologists feature regularly in public discourse at all levels. They appear on radio and television, write for or are interviewed by newspapers, take part in various public debates inside and outside the academic system, and publish popular books and essays. Let us therefore look briefly at some examples of anthropologists' recent interventions in the Norwegian public sphere, just to indicate the range of possible forms of participation.

The annual secondary school students' graduation involves protracted partying in public spaces, reaching a climax of sorts around 17 May, Constitution Day. The pupils, just old enough to drive and drink (although not simultaneously and certainly not in Norway), buy dilapidated old buses repainted red with risqué bons-mots and a few paid ads painted in white. Every year, concerned journalists report that 'this year's partying is wilder and more irresponsible than ever before'. Some years ago, an Oslo newspaper had the excellent idea of interviewing the Argentine anthropologist Eduardo Archetti, who has lived in Norway for many years, about the phenomenon. One of his own children left school that year. Archetti explained, among other things, that for the nineteen year-olds in question, this would be the first time they participated in rituals involving sex and alcohol, which was the main reason that the event was so controversial and saturated with powerful, earthy symbolism. This was not exactly a message to reassure other parents perhaps, but he certainly introduced a new perspective, and an entirely anthropological one, on a phenomenon which usually elicited predictable, worried comments from social scientists.

While I was collecting material for this book, one day I happened to listen to the car radio and heard a familiar voice discoursing on the role of coffee in informal socializing. I recognized the voice as that of Runar Døving, who had recently defended his Ph.D. in anthropology, later published as a book (Døving 2004), on food and society in a coastal hamlet less than two hours out of Oslo. He described some of the typical contexts where coffee was served, adding that if you refuse someone's offer of a cup of coffee, it had better be that you're allergic or it's too late in the evening, and you are then expected to accept tea instead. He spoke at some length about the role of coffee at work (every Norwegian workplace has a semi-public space with a coffee machine) and claimed that without coffee, a great number of social encounters would simply not take place. In another programme in the series, Døving described, drawing on Mauss's classic analysis of reciprocity (Mauss 1954 [1924]), the typical outraged reaction if a house guest politely refused coffee, tea, beer, soft drinks and so on, insisting that she 'just wanted a glass of water'.

Yet another anthropologist, Unni Wikan, has for years argued passionately for human rights and the right to individual choice among minority girls. In her book *Mot en Ny Norsk Underklasse?* [Towards a New Norwegian Underclass] (Wikan 1995; rewritten in English as *Generous Betrayal*, 2001), Wikan argues that muddled thinking informed by wishy-washy multiculturalism and misplaced cultural relativism has deprived many second-generation girls of rights that would have been self-evident for ethnic Norwegian girls. She has often written in newspapers and appeared in other media to express her views, has advised political parties, and has encountered both support and criticism from others, including anthropologists and minority researchers. The many thousands of Norwegians who follow minority issues with an interest above average have over the years got the distinct, and correct, impression that the anthropologists in this country represent differing views about the group–individual relationship, and accordingly hold different views regarding policy.

Again, as I was collecting material for this book, anthropologists were in the national media at least three times in as many days. First, a couple of prominent sport executives proposed that one should pick out the talent at a younger age than presently, in order to improve the country's competitive edge. Anthropologist Jo Helle-Valle was interviewed in this context, and later cited by commentators. Helle-Valle, who was then carrying out research on children's sports (and had himself been a children's football coach), argued that there is no indication that talent in a sport like football is evident before puberty. He also had a few things to say about the role of sport in children's social life. Second, a Ph.D. student who had just defended his thesis about transnational football fans, Hans Hognestad, was interviewed on a full page of a Saturday daily, by a journalist who clearly understood what his research was about. Hognestad could point out, among other things, that the international fan club of Liverpool had more members in Norway than any Norwegian fan club; and that this might tell us something about group allegiance and the transnational potential of sport loyalties. Thirdly, on the very same day I had an article about ethnicity and 'human nature' in Norway's largest daily, reprinted in the last chapter.

It is not considered a professional duty for Norwegian anthropologists to engage with the public. Some raise their voice only rarely, to comment on issues where they are specialists or where they deem that important values are at stake. Thus, in the early days of the 2001 US-led invasion of Afghanistan, Fredrik Barth appeared on radio and wrote a newspaper article discussing what the Western powers might realistically expect to achieve if they tried to impose a Western-type democracy on Afghanistan. He was one of the few people in Norway with the professional authority to do so, and although Barth rarely appears in the media, he has a perceptible impact when he does. In fact, Barth was in his day something of a pioneer for a public anthropology in Norway. In the late 1970s, a TV series was made featuring Barth, where (as I remember it) he spent most of the time sitting behind his desk at the Ethnographic Museum, showing slides and talking about his fieldwork. The series was utterly captivating, it was swiftly transformed into a bestselling book (Barth 1980), and converted not a few young spectators to the magic of anthropology – in its way doing the same kind of work as Granada's *Disappearing Worlds* series did in the UK.

However, in the recent history of Norwegian public anthropology, the one person who stands out is Arne Martin Klausen, who was a professor at the University of Oslo for decades until his retirement in the late 1990s. Klausen's first field of intervention was development assistance, where he criticized – both in academic and in public forums – the tendency among donor organizations to neglect the cultural dimension. He would later publish studies of Norwegian society, and the book he edited in 1984, *Den Norske Væremåten* [The Norwegian Way of Being], had a decisive impact on public debate about 'Norwegianness'. The chapters dealt with topics such as the local community as totem, equality as a key value and conflict-avoidance. Tellingly, there was nothing about hybridity, creolization or immigrants in the book. A decade later, such an omission would have been perceived as a mortal sin.

Klausen, who led a group of researchers studying the 1994 Winter Olympics as a ritual celebrating modernity (Klausen 1999), always maintained in his lectures that anthropologists should be relativists away and critics at home. He sees anthropology as a generalist's discipline opposed to the fragmenting specialization typical of knowledge production in differentiated modern societies. In a word, Klausen tried to teach a generation of anthropologists that they should be quintessential intellectuals: their job at home consisted in approaching society from a slanted angle, writing and saying unexpected and sometimes unpopular things, adding width and depth to society's self-reflection.

I will not attempt to give a full explanation of Norwegian exceptionalism, nor should it be exaggerated. Other countries have their public intellectuals who fill similar niches, and the situation in Norway may be a result of fortuitous historical coincidences. It is nonetheless worth noting that in 1995, a leading journalist in *Aftenposten*, the academically educated Håkon Harket, introduced a lengthy article with the claim that while every social commentator in the 1970s seemed to think like a sociologist, they were now 'carrying an embryonic anthropologist inside': anthropological ideas about cultural difference, the significance of ethnicity, the modernity of contemporary tradition and the sins of ethnocentrism had somehow seeped into the collective psyche. (In other countries, they might blame postmodernism for similar ailments.) Yet Norway is unusual for having a broad palette of publicly active anthropologists covering a wide range of topics. The real embarrassment is that anthropology, so uniquely positioned to make sense of our world, is all but invisible almost everywhere else.

The Multicultural Minefield

Anthropologists have, over the years, intervened occasionally in public debates about multiculturalism and its dilemmas, not merely as specialists offering facts about this or that group, but as generalizts making assessments of a situation on the background of a certain way of thinking and a certain range of knowledge. Sometimes they have participated as political actors in their own right as well, defending or attacking particular policies or moral stances, as Unni Wikan has done in her *Generous Betrayal* (Wikan 2001), a critical book about multiculturalism. The boundary between the learned academic showering the public sphere with a drizzle of knowledge and the engaged intervener is often spurious in practice, however, and anthropologists who want to take part in a less sheltered public sphere than the one they have been socialized into, might as well get used to being co-opted, misunderstood and misrepresented. Because it is bound to happen anyway. Yet, it can be argued, this is usually balanced by the benefits.

An anthropologist at the University of Uppsala, Sweden, Mikael Kurkiala took his Ph.D. research on identity politics among Oglala Lakota in South Dakota. Yet his most important intervention in the media to date did not concern Native Americans or even indigenous peoples, but it is nonetheless obvious that his minute analysis of the twists and turns of their discourse on cultural identity was brought to bear on his articles (see Kurkiala 2003 for a summary of the Swedish media debate).

In January 2002, a Swedish woman of Kurdish origin, Fadime Sahindal, was shot dead by her father. Sahindal, twenty-six years old and a sociology student, was something of a national celebrity, and had often appeared in the media to explain why it was important for her to oppose the patriarchal traditions of her family and to insist on the right to live her life like any other Swede. There was shock and tremendous public outrage in Sweden, in fact in all of Scandinavia. The tragedy, which happened only a few months after 9/11, served as a powerful catalyst to debates about minorities, Islam and immigration in general. In neighbouring Norway and Denmark, the 'Fadime affair' strengthened an already strong opinion against certain aspects of 'immigrant culture', notably the norms and practices limiting the personal freedom of young Muslim women of the second generation. In Sweden, public reactions were more cautious. Anxious not to be taken hostage to xenophobic groups, politicians and public commentators denied that Fadime's murder had anything to do with Kurdish culture or Islam. Some even attributed the murder to universal patriarchy. At the same time, male Kurdish intellectuals in

Sweden, also denying that there was any connection with Kurdish culture, described the father as mentally deranged.

However, a third view soon appeared, one which would have been supremely compatible with anthropology had the murder taken place in a more innocent time or a more distant place. Several contributors to the press, all of them women from areas where honour killings occur, argued that Fadime's murder had an undeniable cultural dimension which needed to be addressed. Far from essentialising Kurdish culture or Islam, they pointed out that in many parts of the world, male control over female sexuality is routinely sanctioned by violence.

At this point, Kurkiala wrote an article in Sweden's leading daily newspaper, *Dagens Nyheter,* where he expressed concern that these women's views were not taken seriously. Indeed, he argued, Fadime's own analysis of her situation, which was not only that of a Swedish woman of Kurdish origin, but also of a sociology student, had actually given priority to cultural factors.

Kurkiala was immediately attacked for allowing himself to function as a useful idiot for the new right and their cultural racism. Responding in an article where he pointed out that in fact, honour killings are real and based on actual cultural traditions, Kurkiala was eventually led to reflect on the fate of the culture concept. If you cannot, as an anthropologist, identify cultural differences without being accused of new racism, the motivation to leave the ivory tower becomes even weaker than it already is.

The problem evident in Kurkiala's entanglement with the Swedish public sphere highlights a difference between the rushed media debate and the intellectual debate, which must insist on its place in the media in spite of its slowness. Of course, Kurkiala did not intimate that Fadime's father was culturally determined to kill his daughter for having brought shame on the family, but that this option was readily available, as one of several possible scripts, in his Kurdish cultural background. But public sentiment after Fadime's death was heated and passionate, there was little time to develop complex positions, and Kurkiala was inadvertently turned into a cardboard cut-out.

The example is unusual in that anthropologists who intervene on similar issues normally issue warnings against facile cultural essentialism; Kurkiala's role was the opposite. Our job in these cases probably consists in defending what Michael Herzfeld has spoken of as the 'militant middle ground'.

Another recent incident involved both the media, a group generally considered vulnerable and subaltern, namely Somali woman refugees, and an anthropologist specializing in East Africa. Following a controversial television documentary about female circumcision, which documented that the practice existed among certain immigrants in Norway, a journalist with the largest Norwegian newspaper, *VG,* decided to write an opinion piece on the issue. She duly contacted Aud Talle, who had done fieldwork in Kenya, Tanzania, Somalia, and among Somali women in

London. Talle faxed her an article describing the social and cultural embeddedness of the practice, as well as explaining the practice on the phone. Soon after, *VG* published an article on female circumcision illustrated by an image of a veiled, chained woman trotting behind a brisk and confident female anthropologist. The story objected to the 'cultural relativism' of the anthropologists, who preferred to study circumcision as an exotic rite rather than trying to combat it.

At first, Talle was uncertain as to how she should react. Eventually she decided not to write a response in the newspaper itself. The fast media, she reckoned, were simply unable to accommodate the kind of detail necessary in an account which had to take all the relevant factors into consideration. So she wrote a book instead, *Om Kvinneleg Omskjering* [On Female Circumcision] (Talle 2003). The book was published a year after the newspaper commentary, and it is written in a popular style. It ends with a few policy recommendations, where Talle makes an interesting comparison between North-East African female circumcision and Chinese foot-binding, suggesting that the successful campaign against the latter practice a hundred years ago might inspire similar strategies today. Her main arguments are the ones insiders might expect from a social anthropologist, and which are, incidentally, rare in general public debate: circumcision has to be understood as an individual experience, but also in terms of cultural meaning and social interests.

Predictably, Talle's book was not reviewed by *VG* nor by any of the other main-stream media. But it had its share of attention in the small elite media, and – more importantly – it began to be used by health workers and public servants, who are often reminded of their need to understand why certain immigrants do certain things. This example shows how anthropologists can function as speed bumps in the public sphere; why it sometimes pays to be patient. Talle's book has an expected longevity which exceeds *VG* articles by years.

The Geniuses and the Idiots

My third example, which illustrates both the necessity and the difficulties of involving oneself in the fast media debates over identity politics and multiculturalism, takes as its point of departure the ongoing debate about immigrants, the second generation, enforced marriages, culture and rights. Such issues have been at the forefront of Scandinavian public attention since the mid-1990s.

In the summer of 2002, a controversy erupted in major Norwegian media, which not only involved social anthropologists, but which also lent itself to a critical interrogation of the possible roles for academics in public arenas. Like many public controversies, it introduced few new arguments or facts about society, but largely consisted in a vigorous exchange of insults, arguments about form and symbolic power, juxtaposing – in the words of one of the contributors to the debate – 'the dusty professors' with 'the young female rebel'.

This is how the story began. It was late July, and we were on holiday in the Lofoten archipelago. The islands are right in the middle of the Gulf Stream, but the Sunday weather was horrible, with torrential rain and strong winds. Our whale-watching trip had been cancelled, to our great disappointment. Waiting for a ferry, we bought a newspaper to check on the weather at home, which – unsurprisingly – was sunny and hot. Idly opening the paper on page four, my wife discovered that half of it consisted of a photo of her husband in front of a bookshelf and a batik print of a Hindu deity, gesturing and apparently saying something to the photographer. Glancing over her shoulder, I could see at once that the article, entitled 'The geniuses and the idiots', did not bring good news. Not to me anyway.

The rain continued to pour, the ferry was late, and I read the article. The author, a columnist and standup comedian named Shabana Rehman, was lashing out against 'the intellectuals', using me as her main punchball, for being irrelevant, patronising and arrogant. Now, the background of this unexpected attack, printed in *Dagbladet*, the largest left-liberal newspaper in the country, was a piece I had published a week or so earlier in a much smaller medium, the highbrow weekly *Morgenbladet*. That newspaper had in turn printed an article attacking academics and so-called leftist intellectuals for sheepishness, 'political correctness' and naive anti-racism in their dealings with both immigrant and minority issues and with the aftermath of 9/11. As one of the intellectuals implicitly attacked (and perhaps not so implicitly; the writer is likely to have had me in mind when he spoke condescendingly about 'pop anthropologists'), I responded with an angry article which argued that virtually everything he said was wrong. There had always been conflicting views and perspectives in research and public debate on migration and ethnic relations; and hardly anybody commenting on 9/11 believed, as this writer alleged, that Osama bin Laden was a spokesman for the impoverished and oppressed of the world.

In the article, I also claimed that these views (about the conformist 'political correctness' in academia) had mysteriously become commonplace, and that a myth had been established during the last year or so, claiming that before the appearance of Shabana Rehman, the debate about multi-ethnic society had been dominated by conservative cultural relativism. This was not intended to belittle her role in Norwegian society – her liberal individualist views, so different from mainstream immigrant views and so compatible with the Zeitgeist, had been very influential and had the definite merit of making simplistic notions of 'the immigrant' problematical.

Rehman's subsequent attack on me, and by extension on all academics, accused us of despising people who had read fewer books than us, being cocooned in the ivory tower, and finally of having conformist views and no influence in greater society. To give a flavour of the engagement displayed in her article, here is a sample near the end:

The elite to which Eriksen belongs just wants to 'know' more and more, and paradoxically, they will encounter growing problems in being understood. Therefore, they will never contribute to any social change. Besides, their main concern is to get a reputation as 'masters of understanding'. The intellectuals chiefly wish to revel in others' admiration of their knowledge. I sure feel they should be allowed to do this, but it ought to take place in a confined room in an ivory tower, especially designated for this activity. (Rehman in *Dagbladet*, 28 July 2002)

That evening I got a text message on my cellphone from a couple of friends – my Oslo publisher and his art historian wife – who advised me not to respond. Since Rehman's accusations were obviously over the top, they said, I ought to keep my counsel.

Returning to Oslo a few days later, I failed to heed their advice and sent a short comment to the newspaper, rectifying some of the errors in the Sunday article. Among other things, I wrote: 'Pointing out factual errors in the accounts of others seems to be synonymous with arrogant elitism in Shabana Rehman's world', but added that 'She has been courageous and uncompromising, and has deservedly received admiration and recognition' (Eriksen in *Dagbladet*, 3 August 2002).

However, by the time this letter was printed, the debate had already taken a new direction. A couple of days earlier, the social anthropologist Marianne Gullestad published a lengthy article in the erstwhile broadsheet *Aftenposten*, where she critically interrogated Rehman's role in Norwegian public life, claiming that her extensive media presence 'overshadowed others'. More substantially, she argued that Rehman's emphasis, in her regular column, on issues such as sexuality and lifestyle, had contributed to shifting public attention away from ethnic discrimination towards less important matters. She also intimated that Rehman's views could easily be appropriated by people who demanded cultural assimilation from immigrants. Perhaps most importantly, she argued that Rehman's position as a liberal, 'liberated' young woman of the second generation confirmed Norwegian stereotypes rather than questioning them, and finally, she lamented her explicit anti-intellectualism – in her original Sunday article, Rehman had claimed that intellectuals were only interested in recognition from other intellectuals, not in influencing or changing society.

Gullestad made a systematic list of ten points (such as 'plays games with Orientalizing effects', 'humour and charisma' and 'confirms negative stereotypes about immigrants') describing Rehman's effects on the Norwegian public sphere, the way she saw it, and went on to analyse why she was so phenomenally popular in the liberal media. The reason, to put it more bluntly than Gullestad did in her very polite article, was that Rehman functioned as a female 'Uncle Tom' or, as they say in Britain, a 'coconut' – black on the outside, white on the inside. However, Gullestad's initial article was quite balanced. It praised Rehman for her courage and originality, but ultimately castigated her for confirming common Norwegian stereotypes. *Aftenposten* had changed her original headline to 'Rehman overshadows others', thereby stressing the conflict potential.

In the following days, both *Aftenposten* and *Dagbladet* published commentaries and interviews with academics, activists and prominent immigrants, who presented a variety of views on the controversy. Some said that Rehman's offensive language (among other things, she has described obedient Muslim women as 'a herd of cows') led to an unhealthy polarization between 'liberals' and 'conservatives' in immigrant circles, making it difficult to build bridges by sustaining more soft-spoken and compromising positions; some defended her against the onslaught from the ivory tower; some attacked the media for not allowing a greater variation in perspectives; and a few confessed ambivalence.

Moreover, both newspapers published several new articles by both Gullestad and Rehman, where they partly repeated their criticisms, partly tried to explain what they 'really meant', and partly expressed dismay at the rhetorical devices employed by their adversary. Interestingly, people with foreign-sounding names almost unanimously supported Gullestad, who was in turn attacked vigorously by most ethnic Norwegians who had their say, including feminist academics.

The controversy does not only pertain to debates over identity politics involving anthropologists jostling for attention in that noisy crowd which makes up the public sphere in any healthy society. Like the Swedish example, it also brings up some general issues to be taken into account for anthropologists (and other academics) who wish to influence opinion in their country.

Symbolic Power Relations.   Different intellectual and political agendas are set in different arenas. The strategy of the columnist-activist is to create maximum attention within a minimum of time, through a well orchestrated intervention phrased in powerful words. In canvassing for public attention on the issue of enforced marriage, Rehman herself had succeeded superbly in this the previous winter. Academics develop and defend their symbolic power in slower and more cumbersome ways, as it takes decades for their capital to accumulate. Their public authority rests not on the felicitious turn of phrase, but on their implied professional expertise. In this debate, both parties seem to have suspected the other of trying to monopolize symbolic power where their arenas intersect, namely in mediated attempts to influence public opinion and policy. Just consider the difference in language. Gullestad wrote, in her first article:

> She courageously challenges patriarchal and authoritarian ways of thinking among 'immigrants', but [does] not [address] typical prejudices in the Norwegian establishment. (Gullestad, *Aftenposten*, 1 August 2002)

Rehman angrily responded the next day, in *Dagbladet*:

> For a long time, I thought fundamentalist imams and politicians were subverting the open debate about equity and the multi-ethnic society. But now I realize that it is ethnically

> Norwegian women like ... social anthropologist Marianne Gullestad who really sabotage the debate. (Rehman, *Dagbladet*, 2 August 2002)

While Gullestad comes across as mild and equivocal, Rehman's texts brim with righteous anger at the 'politically correct mantras' of minority experts, their cowardly relativism and their patronising attitude:

> Had I only smiled and nodded politely, lived in an arranged marriage with my cousin and covered my hair, spoken broken Norwegian and told stories about that idiotic neighbour hag who forces me to scrub the stairs, then I would have served as an acceptable example for Marianne Gullestad. (Rehman, ibid.)

Deliberately provocative, Rehman here suggests that Gullestad and her ilk want immigrant women to be oppressed by Norwegians to fit a master story about racism and intolerance. Gullestad responded, a couple of days later:

> I hope that in the future, the Norwegian public sphere will ... be able to accommodate experiences from many more points of view than mine and that of Shabana Rehman. (Gullestad, *Aftenposten*, 4 August 2002)

Impeccably polite, Gullestad adopts the bird's-eye view. She presents herself not as someone whose duty it is to intervene on her own behalf, but as a person who coolly defends the rights of the people Rehman had described as 'a herd of cows'. Rehman, on her part, draws on her own experience as a young woman with a Muslim background, arguing that people like Gullestad have been useful idiots for reactionary forces.

It is not easy to see which of them carries the most symbolic power in a public sphere where the authority of academics has already been undermined. Rehman, who in her later articles said that she was not an anti-intellectual, but wanted the intellectuals (that is academics) to be more relevant and closer to the life experiences of 'real people', went on to offer arguments familiar from feminist and human rights groups in India and the Muslim world. Gullestad argued that there were lots of 'real people' who were not represented in Rehman's universe. Both had important points to make, but their frames of reference were different.

Social Responsibility. Both the academic and the non-academic who were acting out this controversy profess humanist, political or moral intentions. Rehman evidently sees herself as a champion of universal human rights; Gullestad, an engaged intellectual who has often intervened through the Norwegian media, is concerned with the respect for and recognition of a multitude of experiences and life-worlds. There are some fundamental differences between their ontologies (Rehman being strongly individualist – some would even say voluntarist – while Gullestad emphasizes the social and relational in the shaping of persons), but that is not the point here. Their views on social responsibility are similar, but they diverge politically as well as in their respective views on proper form.

There is an often neglected class dimension to this kind of conflict. It can be argued that academics and their benignly condescending middle-class world-view reduce others to puppets. This would be Rehman's view. In Gullestad's view, Rehman's tendency to 'shoot from the hip' alienates and offends people who are in their right to subscribe to other values and live other kinds of lives.

Scholarly Responsibility. This set of obligations applies in at least two ways: academics are responsible for not misrepresenting their research object in public, and for protecting the integrity of their informants. Both kinds of responsibility militate against their presenting their findings in the mass media. Journalists are less constrained. A columnist represents only herself and can tell any story she likes. In a TV documentary revealing that several Muslim leaders in Norway defended the practice of female circumcision, they were filmed with a hidden camera, and the interviewer was a young African woman who asked to be taken into their confidence, never revealing that she was a journalist. Such methods could never have been used by social anthropologists, and our ethical guidelines reduce our potential for generating juicy tabloid fodder.

The Norwegian journalist Åsne Seierstad's international bestseller *The Bookseller of Kabul*, incidentally, brought up similar ethical issues in the Norwegian press in 2003 (Myhre 2004). In her book, Seierstad had presented the main protagonist, the Afghani bookshop owner, without trying to conceal his identity (as if it had been possible – there are a limited number of well-stocked bookshops in Kabul, to put it mildly). By revealing facts and retelling intimate stories given to her in confidentiality by family members, and by representing her main character in a largely unflattering way, she satisfied the sensibilities of her North Atlantic feminist readers, but seems to have compromised the trust placed in her by her hosts. The bookseller eventually got to see a draft English translation of the book, passed to him not by Seierstad or her publisher, but by a third party. He was outraged and announced his intention of suing for libel. An anthropologist would necessarily have treated her informants differently and created fewer headlines.

The Social Construction of Academic Reality. In one of her contributions to the debate with Gullestad, Rehman wrote that academics live in a 'goldfish bowl'. This view was subsequently supported by many of the contributors to online debates, who claimed that academic researchers knew little about 'the real world'. Instead of confronting messy realities and dangerous political issues, Rehman and others have alleged, they politely and respectfully exchange views in the closed circles of the academy, risking little by way of exposure to the less polished voices 'from the people' or the merciless machinery of the mass media. This may be correct, but academics would be likely to respond that their job is documentation and analysis, possibly influencing politics by producing commissioned reports; and that they have no obligation to be visible in the news media. Heaven knows, as Gullestad remarked, we all live in our goldfish bowls. Yet Rehman's view needs to be taken seriously. There is a middle-class aloofness in the standard academic way of engaging, evident even among those of us who do take the risk of sticking their necks out, and by not taking personal risks (as Rehman certainly has done), academics can easily be accused of complacency and cowardice. There are times when one is obliged to shout one's heresies rather than whispering one's doubts.

Form, Content and Efficacy. The debate, which largely took place in two major Norwegian newspapers (but was commented upon in other media), was characterized by *extreme speed*. By the time I published my very short response to Rehman's attack, less than a week after it was printed, the focus of the controversy had already changed, and my comments seemed dated. Few academics would have been able to follow the speed, and to not feel intimidated by the massive media pressure, entailed by the controversy. As Marianne Gullestad remarked some time afterwards, following several weeks of almost daily attacks on her work, her views and/or her person: Who is going to feel tempted to stick their neck out now?

There is no simple lesson to be learnt about anthropologists as public intellectuals here. Surely, the Rehman–Gullestad controversy can be understood as a confrontation between two partly overlapping language games. The language game where Rehman is at home exhorts the player to be witty, provocative, fast and personally engaged. Gullestad's language game is regulated by rules that require logical consistency, conscientious and balanced presentation of the evidence, unambiguous language, and loyalty to the exposed subjects. However, the media allow both (and other) language games to coexist, but there is little doubt that the former has a more considerable public impact than the latter.

Interestingly, the most common complaint among scholars and researchers who feel misrepresented in the media, namely that their views are simplified and misunderstood (Eriksen 2003b), does not seem to apply here. Both Gullestad and the other academics who participated in this controversy were given ample space to elaborate their views – this was, after all, early August, a notoriously quiet period of the year, newswise, the 'cucumber season' in Norwegian parlance, that is a period when newspapers are desperate enough to print stories about unusually large or misshapen cucumbers, displayed by the proud children of local farmers. Still, the contrast between speed and simplification on the one hand, and slowness and complexity on the other, is evident as a contextual factor. In the commentary that started the debate (although this was soon forgotten), I had criticized a newspaper article for not offering a shred of evidence for its sweeping statements, thus requesting a slower and more cautious way of dealing with the world. In one of her responses to Gullestad, Rehman wrote that at the time when the murder of a young, second-generation Swedish woman by her father (Fadime) was all over the news, 'the academics' were busy debating whether or not Norwegians had become more racist over the past decade. In her response to this, Gullestad explained that she had been working on the book in question for four years, which is to say that it belonged to a slower temporal regime than the flickering daily news.

The contrast pertains to academic and journalistic ways of presenting an argument. However, the debate says little about the situation of social anthropology as such. Similar exchanges might take place between cautious researchers and impatient activists in many other areas, for example relating to environmental issues, GM foods or international politics.

So how does anthropology come into it, if at all? I think it does, and if our strength consists in seeing the world from below and from the inside, and in representing (in both meanings of the word) voices which are sometimes muted, then Marianne Gullestad does just this when she reminds the Norwegian newspaper readers that there are many other stories, experiences and life-worlds among members of first-, second- and third-generation minorities, than the ones told by *Dagbladet*'s powerful columnist. But whereas Gullestad's call for nuance and pluralism subverts a monolithic set of ideas about the good life, Rehman's angry accusations of betrayal are uncomfortable reminders of the middle-class aloofness allowing anthropologists to keep social conflicts in their own society at arm's length. In the last analysis, the Rehman–Gullestad shoot-out was not so much about ethnicity as about class; certainly in content and possibly in form as well.

Speed Versus Slowness

This chapter has been about speed and slowness in mass communication. Kurkiala's views were distorted by speed, while Talle refused to participate in the fast game and insisted on slowing down. It takes Shabana Rehman, an intelligent and powerful writer, ten seconds to say, to general acclaim, that the emperor is naked (Hey, why don't you think we brown women should be free?). The anthropologists' response has consisted in slowing down, spreading out their cards one by one, patiently explaining that the real world is more variegated and real lives less easy to judge than slogan-like headlines imply.

Like other intellectuals, anthropologists can function as speed-bumps in this kind of landscape, and that is an important part of their job. In this regard, perhaps we should simply accept and endorse our middle-class habitus and its therapeutic effect on heated controversy? This may be worth considering. Yet, nothing is gained if we are only able to serve as speed-bumps for each other. My view is that when anthropologists take on identity politics, they should not shy away from unabashed moral-political engagement. They could also be bolder in their comparisons, notwithstanding dismissive views of the ahistorical 'anthropological gambit'. If an anthropologist says, as he might well do, that studies of stateless societies in Central Africa can shed light on the civil war in Bosnia, he is likely to get an audience. The moment the readers are hooked, they can be seduced into following that cumbersome, cautious way of reasoning which is necessary in order to move beyond the clichés. I also think we could make more of the mental unity of humanity; give it some content. Surely there must be some traces of human universals in the way people go about dealing with difference under shifting circumstances? This is probably where we should ultimately look for simple answers, in human nature. But one must not get there too fast.

An important difference between anthropological writing and journalism is that anthropologists tend to postpone the climax until the concluding paragraphs of the text, while journalists are taught to grab the reader's attention in the first sentence. Attention spans are supposed to be short, and shrinking, in this era of fast, abundant communication. It has also been claimed, with some supportive documentation, that contemporary Westerners generally speak faster, use shorter words and a language poorer in nuance and vocabulary, than the previous generations. Debatable as these views are, it is doubtless one of the intellectual's tasks to function as a speed-bump. Whenever the intellectual tries to play the game of the fast media, frictions between temporal regimes develop, and this is how it should be.

However, it should be kept in mind that there are many media in the space between the tabloid and the specialist monograph. Radio is generally slower than television. Magazines published by organizations for the benefit of their members are also less sensation-seeking and polarizing than the mass circulation media, since the members share some interests and receive the magazine regardless of the cover story. Over the years, I have contributed to such magazines quite often, occasionally as a regular columnist for a year or two. The column reprinted below appeared in *Amnesty-Nytt* [Amnesty News], the newsletter of the Norwegian branch of Amnesty International. Intended for the educated and above-average interested readership of *Amnesty-Nytt*, the article was not meant to question the individualism of human rights principles, but to criticize the inadequate sociological understanding characteristic of some of the more facile attacks on cultural practices and notions among immigrants.

Neo-liberalism and the Minorities

There have been changes in the way we talk about multi-ethnic society. This has not just taken place here, incidentally; in all of Western Europe, there has occurred a gradual shift in recent years, especially after 11 September 2001, in the dominant framework regulating exchanges of views about immigrants and natives.

Two changes are particularly noticeable. First, there has been a shift from a sociological focus on discrimination and racism, towards a focus on repression and rights violations inside the minority communities. Second, the anthropological emphasis on cultural rights (associated with language, religious practices etc.) has been replaced almost completely by public debate regarding individual rights and choice as unquestioned values, even in extreme quantities. Freedom values replace security values, and the burden of evidence is pushed from greater society across to the immigrants theselves. The stigmatizing Progress Party [right-wing populist party] term 'culturally alien' (*fremmedkulturell*) has entered the everyday vocabulary of the press in spite of warnings from both academics and journalists. The blanket term 'immigrant community' has become synonymous with oppression and dark powers. The tragic Fadime affair last winter demonstrated to the public sphere once and for all that groups are evil (at least if they are culturally alien), and what now matters is to speed up and intensify 'integration' (read Norwegianization).

Both tendencies are connected to neo-liberalist ideology, which transcends conventional political divides and is as widespread in the Labour Party as in the Progress Party. This is the ideology which, among other things, promotes maximal individual freedom of choice and the adjustment of public services to render them more efficient and their institutions more compatible with market-economic common sense.

Neo-liberalism is not in itself xenophobic. Quite the opposite: it is a doctrine of freedom which promotes open borders and free competition. However, it is based on a view of what it is to be human which conforms badly with reality in ways which can stimulate xenophobic attitudes.

We are talking about an unreformed (and unreflected) individualism where the only thing the individual owes his surroundings is self-realization. This individualism carries with it conventional criteria of success – money, power, public visibility. Moreover, it implies that groups either do not exist ('There is no such thing as society') or create obstacles to the individual's freedom.

The ideological shift has led to a change in emphasis in the standard presentation of minority issues (enforced marriages rather than discrimination in the labour market; unwillingness to integrate among immigrants rather than demands for cultural rights), and entails that greater society is either regarded as non-existent or devoid of responsibilities – it is up to the individuals themselves to sort out their lives – and cultural institutions in minority groups become disturbing elements; they curtail individual freedom and reduce the efficiency of Norway Ltd.

As a part of the new rhetoric, it has become a common exercise among commentators to denounce the 'kindness policy' of the last generation. Since both female circumcision and enforced marriages demonstrably occur among immigrants (however rarely), and researchers have devoted relatively little attention to such phenomena, myths have been spun and disseminated quickly and efficiently about powerful alliances of NGOs' networks, researchers and high-ranking bureaucrats who have refused to face realities, and who have instead built a castle in the sky called 'the rainbow society'. This image is a caricature.

On the other hand, it is correct that it was until quite recently common to accept the validity of a structural understanding of problems associated with migration; that is, one could not just blame individual decisions or shortcomings, personal idiosyncracies and so on. Someone who belongs to a minority is entitled to both freedom and security. He or she can take decisions, and greater society is obliged to ensure that the choices are real. For example, it ought to be possible, not just in theory but also in practice, for rural and working-class youths to take higher education if they want to, and it similarly ought to be possible for a young woman with Pakistani parents to refuse to marry the man her parents have chosen for her.

At the same time, it would be ignorant and dangerous to deny that important aspects of the social world we inhabit have not been chosen, neither by ourselves nor by anybody else. We do not choose our early childhood experiences, our kin, our class background or our mother tongue. Crucial experiences vary and imply that each of us makes decisions on differing premises. To some of us it is not even certain that the decisions or choices are the most important things in life; maybe we prefer security, predictability and belonging to a group.

There is a genuine predicament here, which incidentally goes right to the core of the foundational problems of social science. On the one hand, society is nothing but the result of a lot of individual choices. On the other hand, these choices are impossible unless there exists a society beforehand, which provides us with a language and a set of values, and identifies which alternatives it is possible to choose between.

Eager to emphasize the freely choosing individual, public debate has almost inadvertently done away with the groups. At the very least, this has happened in the minority debate. All of a sudden, culturally specific experiences and cultural differences have no value in the marketplace of ideas; and if they exist after all, they should be flattened out of consideration for the free choices of individuals. Just a decade ago, it was acceptable to talk about cultural differences in a respectful way, indicating that they had to be understood and acknowledged if the integration of culturally different groups in a single society were to be successful. Differences in child-raising and gender roles provoked and enraged social democratic politicians and social workers, and many were hoping that things would eventually change – but at the same time, everybody involved agreed that it was impossible to remove deep-seated cultural practices by decree. Such changes come about slowly and gradually, as people acquire new experiences and notions.

This kind of insight has become rare. The public sphere thus sees only shortcomings and evil intentions when confronted with cultural differences. 'The others' have again become inferior, as they were in the past. This time, however, they are not inferior as a race or a cultural group, but exclusively as individuals, who oppress each other, who tacitly allow themselves to be oppressed, and who have nothing to complain about in their relationship to majority society, since as everybody knows by now, the anti-Norwegian sentiment among immigrants is much more serious than xenophobic attitudes among ethnic Norwegians. (As if that would make a difference! A simple calculation would show that even if this view were correct, immigrants encounter prejudice more often than Norwegians, simply because there are fewer of them. They meet Norwegians far more often than Norwegians meet immigrants.)

The new, cynical way of talking about minorities and rights in Norway is not, in other words, a result of old-fashioned nationalism. The latter was a kind of collectivism which could occasionally propose compromise and peaceful coexistence with other groups. It nevertheless had its obvious weaknesses, which could only be addressed properly via a strong antidote of no-nonsense individualism. However, the pendulum has now swung so far in the opposite direction that concepts such as 'ethnic group' or 'cultural minority' are immediately associated with enforced marriages and authoritarian religion. In this kind of situation, entire life-worlds are opened to general suspicion and censored.

The only viable solution is one which accepts impurities and locates itself somewhere between security and freedom, between group integration and individuality. Each of them is meaningless without the other, and that is why there can be no easy way out.

This intervention, admittedly written for a cultural elite readership, was an attempt to question a currently taken-for-granted view of 'free choice' and to highlight the fundamental tension between what social scientists call 'agency and structure'. What is missing in this column is documentation. The argument is parasitical on the readers' structures of relevance. Unless the argument rings true with them, it fails for lack of substantial props. Now, to my delight, the next issue of *Amnesty-Nytt* contained an irritated response to my article, penned by a smart woman who asked if all this meant that I held that enforced marriages and other patriarchal practices were acceptable, since they were embedded in cultural experience. A rejoinder followed, enabling me to elaborate further on the issue. In a small way, the exchange showed that civil society continued to function.

Yet it cannot be denied that there are some genuine dilemmas here. Since the late 1980s, I have taken part in more radio and TV programmes than I care to remember; I have done short, long and portrait interviews with all kinds of media, written a great number of columns, book reviews and longer articles in all the major newspapers in Norway and contributed frequently to national newspapers in Denmark and Sweden as well. Obviously, if it were possible, I would have deleted some of these media appearances, especially on television, from historical record. For years, I would defend the view that if you were given one minute on national television to tell your fellow citizens that, say, terrorism has nothing to do with Islam, that 'traditional' Norwegian culture is a modern invention with a commercial face and a political one, or that it is a widespread feeling among immigrants that they get the worst from both worlds; then that single minute would still be better than nothing. Experience now tells me that this is not necessarily the case. Far too often, I have, like Micaela di Leonardo, felt co-opted by the entertainment industry after initially entering the studio expecting a serious debate. Yet, the condescending attitude displayed to many academics towards the mainstream media *as such* is too crude, categorical and misinformed to be helpful. It is also ultimately undemocratic. If people who see themselves as enlightened do not try to shape opinion in their environment, who would they rather leave the task to? Mind you, there is a great difference between talking to a journalist on the phone about why it might be that adults no longer wear pyjamas in our part of the world, and taking part in a forty-minute radio programme about the 2004 tsunami, risk, human rights, the Lisbon earthquake and vulnerability. Trivialization should not be conflated with interventions that might make a difference. And there is an important qualitative difference between writing a 1,000-word article about the shortcomings of genetic determinism and talking for thirty seconds about the same topic on television. In other words, for those who fear the loss of their academic virtue, the question ought not to be for or against public interventions, but rather which kind of intervention through what kind of media. Besides, if we take a large view of things, it is probably better both for the subject's reputation and for the quality of public discourse if some practitioners occasionally make simplistic statements in the media, than if they all remain silent in the wider public sphere. It is easy to blame the contemporary media – shallow, sensationalist, profit-oriented – for the relative absence of anthropologists, but the argument can go both ways: perhaps the unchecked superficiality and triviality of contemporary mass media (especially television), where every issue, no matter how serious, seems to be turned into some form of entertainment, has been able to progress without meeting serious resistance, precisely because intellectuals have been busy talking to each other for the last few decades?

Real dilemmas nevertheless remain. Recently, a political scientist was contacted by a journalist writing a feature story about the situation in Chechnya. The researcher was a regional expert who thought it important to tell the public that the Islamic character of the Chechen uprising was a recent invention; that the Chechen movement was rooted in nineteenth-century, anti-imperial political nationalism. Getting this message across might not just influence citizens' views of the Chechen conflict, but it could also, in a small way, mollify the growing resentment against Islam and Muslims generally. However, it was a busy day, and the researcher had already made her point several times on radio and television during the previous weeks. So she told the journalist that she wasn't keen on talking about it right now. His reply was, 'All right then, s'pose I'll just write something then', implying that without her expert comments, he would have to make his own amateur inferences. So she acquiesced in the end, allowing herself to be blackmailed by the journalist for the sake of the public good.

Apparently, the conversation between the journalist and the intellectual commentator is based on a shared understanding and shared interests in using the media to enlighten the public. In practice, as many members of both groups have experienced, the encounter is often conflictual. The journalist wants conciseness, facts and clear conclusions, and he wants it now. The academic wants to think about the matter for a while, before returning with complexity and ambiguity. The academic also increasingly declines to be an intellectual. Move her two inches outside of her area of specialization, and she becomes silent.

There are many forms of journalism, but as a rule, a journalistic text is structured almost in the opposite way to the academic article, with the main points of the article summarized already in the first paragraph and embellishments, in so far as space admits, below. Academic texts, on the contrary, build up slowly (like the proverbial Indian marriage) and often reveal the whole point of the exercise only in the conclusion. Academics are conditioned not to give everything away at once, and they are naturally often disappointed when they read their quote (typically one to three sentences) in the press. When they are interviewed as experts, they admittedly have little influence on the narrative structure and the overall context in which their statement is framed. Speaking to newspapermen on the phone is a hazardous sport. In their own writings for the general public, however, academics would often benefit from picking up a technique or two from writers who depend on instant consumption and commercial appeal. Anthropology books that succeed in communicating with the general public often draw on striking examples to whet the appetite for more, before offering relatively complex explanations which, if well executed, give the reader the rewarding feeling of having understood something new and difficult. As someone once said of Richard Dawkins, he can make the reader feel like a genius. Now it is often said (not least by academics) that the media world, like the State and the market in their ways, is a black hole of simplification. However, it could also be envisioned as a maelstrom, with quieter waters at the edges, where there is ample space for reflection. Our task, rather than remaining aloof from the crazy world out there, consists in resisting the temptation to simplify too much, not underestimating the intelligence and patience of the readers, and accepting that writing well and oral rhetoric are respectable skills that can be learnt.

–5–

Narrative and Analysis

Everybody wants their work to make a difference, but there is no justice in the world. As Howard Morphy says, following an appreciation of Bill Harney's pioneering ethnographic work among Australian Aborigines, 'in world terms, Harney's works have made no impact whatsoever, whereas [Bruce] Chatwin's *The Songlines* has achieved considerable renown' (1996: 172). To the general reading public, it matters little whether Chatwin used anthropological expert knowledge irresponsibly and according to whim, that his book may be muddled in its reasoning, reactionary in its social attitudes and dangerously old-fashioned in its romantic view of cultural authenticity – most of all, it matters little that most of his insights may be derivative. (His language is not!) According to Morphy, Australian anthropologists disliked Chatwin's book, perhaps – he suggests – because they were themselves his informants. His success was parasitical on their sweat.

The world of public discourse and, beyond that, literary fame, is not fair and just in a Habermasian sense. It doesn't necessarily happen that the best arguments, and the best documented statements, win in the end. Betty Mahmoody's sensationalist novel about patriarchy and broken family relationships, *Not Without My Daughter* (Mahmoody 1989), may in its day have been the main source of information about life in Iran to most reading Americans; Florinda Donner's pseudo-documentary *Shabono* (Donner 1992) has been a bestselling book about the Yanomami; and Nigel Barley remains more widely known in the UK than, say, Marilyn Strathern or Adam Kuper.

Such details may lead anthropologists inclined towards cultural pessimism to believe that one has to be simplistic and moralizing, to present caricatures of the other and to wade in sex, violence, tearful confessions and melodramatic betrayals in order to get the attention of people who are not paid to read whatever it is that one writes. This, fortunately, is far from the truth, and the record of successful popular anthropology books shows otherwise: *The Chrysanthemum and the Sword* (Benedict 1974 [1946]) not only modified American ideas about Japan, but had a profound influence in Japan itself; *Tristes Tropiques* (Lévi-Strauss 1978a) is, in its way, just as complex as *Les Structures Élémentaires de la Parenté* (Lévi-Strauss 1949). Even less ambitious books, such *Cannibals and Kings* (Harris 1978) or *Growing up in New Guinea* (Mead 1930), presumably enriched the readers' perspectives on the world, rather than merely confirming their prejudices, as lesser books do.

A glance at the publishing successes of twentieth-century anthropology in fact suggests that they give little reason to be ashamed on behalf of the guild. Compared to others who write about cultural differences or traditional societies, popularizing anthropologists nearly always succeed in adding complexity and challenging ethnocentric complacency. More often than not, they reveal the humanist origins of their subject by emphasizing the equal value of all human life, thus intimating that knowledge of other cultures or societies can ultimately lead to reform at home. Even the arch-determinist Harris ends his *Cannibals and Kings* on an upbeat note: 'In life, as in any game whose outcome depends on both luck and skill, the rational response to bad odds is to try harder' (Harris 1978: 210).

Anthropology sometimes seems to be perched uncomfortably between two perils: the tyranny of details and the tyranny of models. On the one hand, the serious ethnographer rarely uses one example if five will do; but on the other hand, the mass of examples fails to make sense unless it is structured by a powerful and convincing set of research questions. Yet the feeling remains that anthropology inadvertently dries out the river, unlike history, which brings water to the dry riverbed.

A doctoral student who was also an active musician once approached the legendary avant-garde rock musician Robert Fripp, asking him if he could do an ethnographic study of Fripp's renowned Guitar Craft Seminar. This student was part of the seminar, which was notable for its innovative teaching methods, among them mixing highy skilled players and beginners in the same classes, often with a stunning collective result in performance. Fripp, who did not think highly of academic research, although he admired Victor Turner's work on initiation rituals, hesitated. In the end, he asked the student: 'Why do an academic study when you have the real thing at hand?' In other words: Why dry out the river when you are capable of having a swim?

The student found another empirical field for his doctoral project. (He wrote his thesis on cultural hybridity among youths in Oslo.)

Merely stating that anthropologists dry out the river is not just insulting, but it is also, fortunately, inaccurate. Most anthropologists presumably have a definite audience in mind as they write, but it tends to be so limited that many potential readers are usually not even addressed. Obviously, specialized research should chiefly be disseminated among the specialists and their students, and it would be irrelevant to complain that it is dry and difficult. But equally often, anthropological texts address topic areas, and illuminate questions pertaining to the human condition, which are of burning importance to a great number of non-specialists. By opting for analytical dissection rather than a dramatic narrative with ebbs, flows, counterpoints and constructed climaxes, many anthropologists end up alienating the people they should have reached.

As examples in previous chapters have shown, there are many ways of telling an anthropological story efficiently without compromising its intricacies. In a discussion of popularizing strategies, Sutton (1991) proposes an interesting contrast, inspired by Walter Benjamin, between storytelling and novel-writing. The storyteller 'shares the companionship of his audience, and they can respond and add to his creations.... . The novel, by contrast, is both constructed and consumed in isolation' (Sutton 1991: 92). The implied contrast seems to apply to the difference between the oral and the written, but that would be far too simple. Many of the best writers address their readers as accomplices, as friends or fellow-travellers, or as adversaries to be won over. That was Montaigne's method in *Essais*, and its potential has not been exhausted yet. Arguably, the open-ended storytelling mode would have been appropriate for a discipline like anthropology in its current incarnation, where few final answers are offered and theoretical conclusions tend to be provisional.

We now move to look at a few examples which demonstrate what the contrast between an analytical and a narrative mode may look like in practice. For this chapter, I have chosen the field of identity politics, since it is a subject area where anthropologists have a strong expertise, publish actively and ought to be able to reach a broad or even mass audience now and then. Towards the end, I look at ways in which anthropologists have utilized their knowledge to intervene in global politics, chiefly through the medium of journalism. Now, journalism is fast and anthropology is slow, as discussed earlier. However, journalism is also narrative in ways that anthropology is not. 'Showing, not telling' is a journalistic slogan which sits uncomfortably with the anthropological habitus. This makes for interesting confrontations.

Anthropology and Identity Politics

The debates about cultural pluralism, cultural conflict and fundamentalism, hybrid identities and religious revitalization sometimes seem to be everywhere. One main cluster of debates concerns the relationship between 'Islam and the West'. Gaining prominence after the end of the Cold War, concomitant with the emergence of the symbolically important Rushdie Affair, strengthened by the first Gulf War (which, incidentally, had little or nothing to do with Islam), and boosted enormously a decade later by the 9/11 shock in the USA and European debates about topics such as Muslim headscarves and immigrant policy, there has been a phenomenal increase in public attention towards these issues since the mid-1980s.

Here is a taste of the omnipresence of this topic in the North Atlantic world of the early twenty-first century. Travelling to a symposium on the Dalmatian coast in April 2004, I read an Austrian newspaper on the plane, which ran a feature story on the likelihood of Muslim terrorist attacks in Jordan and other Arab countries. An English newspaper left by a previous passenger contained a report on *hijabs* in Britain and the USA, and the symposium itself occasionally dipped into the topic of identity politics in a wider, comparative sense. Retreating to my room after evening drinks, I perused Orhan Pamuk's novel *Snow*, where the story gravitates around a mysterious string of suicides committed by young hijab-wearing girls in Kars, a city in eastern Turkey. Returning to quiet Oslo after a short week of absence, I discovered that the talk of the town for the last few days had been a woman of Pakistani origin (the Shabana Rehman of the previous chapter), who had performed an impromptu lifting of a Muslim cleric during a public meeting, thereby ridiculing him in public. The question discussed by every columnist in the land during the next couple of weeks was whether she thereby effectively commented on patriarchy and male pomposity in Islam, or if she simply confirmed and strengthened the hegemony of a certain Western view on gender relations and religion. The question was whether the assault on the cleric came from above or from below – or, translated into academic jargon, whether it was a hegemonic act of symbolic domination or a counter-hegemonic one of resistance.

Another approach to identity politics takes new theories of culture as its point of departure. Anthropologists now know these debates like the back of their hand. Following a period when cultures were seen as tightly integrated and based on inside sharing and outside boundaries, criticism of 'monolithic' views of culture mounted in the aftermath of the political radicalization of students in the 1960s, and 'multiple voices', 'cultural hybrids', 'alternative discourses' and similar terms became commonplace. Systematizing a view of culture as the basis for communication rather than the sharing of traits, anthropologists like Ulf Hannerz (1992) developed neo-diffusionist theories of globalization and cultural creolization, while others moved towards the arcane language and sublime insights of postmodernism, where '*il n'y a pas d'hors-texte*'. Pouncing on the new concepts of culture, liberated from the strait-jacket of assumed sharing, stability and homogeneity, ethnographers began to make studies focusing on various forms of mixing, migration, intragroup variation and local varieties of global phenomena such as soap operas and hamburger consumption. In the realm of identity politics, studies of cultural mixing ranged from the sociologically complex (e.g. Baumann 1996) to the culturally surprising (e.g. Çaglar 1999), sometimes pointing out that there is often a dynamic interrelationship between strict patrolling of boundaries and cultural purification on the one hand, and movements towards individualism and self-conscious mixing on the other. Indeed, different members of the same family might opt for different identity strategies; one son in an urban Mauritian family might take great pains to learn about his Tamil tradition, and try to conform to its requirements, while his brother studies in Europe, speaks French, wears Western clothes and cares nothing for the archaic beliefs and customs of his great-grandparents.

One may ask rhetorically: Is anyone better equipped to make sense of these complexities – religion, identification, modernities, migration, mixing – than anthropologists? As always, they can be trusted to make a lot of sense of it. Chiefly to each other, that is. There are textbooks and general overviews written by anthropologists which are useful, not least as a means of socializing students into the subject, but they are unlikely to, and probably not intended to, make the crowds run to get a copy.

The Right Wing According to Holmes

It can be deeply rewarding, but also frustrating, to read what anthropologists have to say about identity politics. In terms of sheer volume, anthropologists have been prolific in the field. Considering variation, the contribution from anthropology is nothing less than daunting. The quality of some of the anthropological work in the area is stunning, combining original theorizing with meticulous attention to detail. An important example is Douglas Holmes' analysis of right-wing populists in England and France, *Integral Europe* (Holmes 2000). The reason it deserves a fairly detailed treatment here is that the book by and large fulfils its extravagant promise, namely to identify and account for the connection between global capitalism and the new right in Europe. Yet it has failed to achieve either the mass readership or the broad intellectual impact it might have had.

Holmes' argument runs roughly like this. Pitting vulnerable groups against each other, the anonymous, but elite-dominated social order channels popular resentment away from fundamental aspects of the economic system through a *divide et impera* manoeuvre. Holmes shows that right-wing populism directed against immigrants is a perfectly understandable reaction among that disenchanted working class which is no longer really needed in society. He also shows how it is linked to the 'new racism', where one's own culture is glorified and presented as being ancient and pure. Faced with rationalist, centralist European integration on the one hand and ruthless, technology-driven global capitalism on the other, large groups discover that their input is no longer necessary, or that they compete for the remaining manual jobs with determined and highly motivated immigrants.

At the same time, Holmes says that the 'flattening' effects of what he calls fast-capitalism and consumerism create a sense of alienation and involuntary uprootedness on a larger scale, a sense that something is lost, which is a feeling also shared by many who are not directly affected by the restructuring of the economy.

Holmes follows other social scientists in developing the gist of his argument. Zygmunt Bauman is quoted approvingly in a passage which states that there are a growing number of people in our North Atlantic societies who are simply no longer needed as 'drawers of water and hewers of wood' or, for that matter, for any other purpose. It has been estimated that in early Edwardian England, the most common occupation in Britain was that of a domestic servant. If anyone except the very rich have servants nowadays, they are likely to be either nineteen-year-old au pairs from another European country or recent immigrants.

The main theoretical source of inspiration for Holmes' work seems to be Isaiah Berlin's work on the counter-Enlightenment (Berlin 1976; see also Gellner 1991).

Now here is an intellectual who has no fear of communicating beyond the guild nor of taking on huge questions! Berlin shows, in his seminal book, how German Romanticism, directed against French domination (and complacent philosophers like Voltaire), cultural nationalism and widespread nostalgia followed in the wake of rationalism and industrialization from the late eighteenth century on. He also shows how these strands permutated into Fascism and Nazism in the early to middle part of the twentieth century, leaving it to people like Holmes to explain how the xenophobic new right is also a true-born child of the counter-enlightenment. There is obviously an important argument here and one which goes much further than to European right-wing populism. Politics feeding on resentment and humiliation are well known all over the world, especially in the poorer areas. Since global capitalism creates both wealth and poverty, the resentment is likely to grow deeper as the globalization of markets intensifies. A book is waiting to be written about the USA as the France of the turn of the millennium, pitted against its Romantic Germany of political Islam and other localist movements.

In the mid-1990s, frustrated with the prejudiced and nationalist perspectives on Europe prevalent in my own country, I wrote a couple of articles (published in a Swedish newspaper, English version available online, Eriksen 1996) which compared the religious puritanism of Algeria's *Front Islamique du Salut* (The Islamic Salvation Front) with the cultural puritanism of the Norwegian 'No to EU' movement. Reading Holmes' superior account made me recall this argument, which identified two very different, yet related instances of anti-Enlightenment sentiment which can be observed virtually everywhere in the global era. So Holmes is unlikely to be correct in identifying the tension between the Enlightenment and counter-Enlightenment with Europe *as such*; in the modern world, it is more universal than that.

I have seen the development of what Holmes describes as fast-capitalism take place in my own city. As late as the early 1980s, there were still a large number of major industrial enterprises in Oslo, and most shops were of the one-of-a-kind category, many of them family-run and carrying names like 'Andersen & Søn'. Incredible as it may sound to Anglo-American readers, we had no franchised fast-food outlets, night shops or nationwide supermarket chains. The property market was uninteresting for investors, and the shops closed at five. A decade later, the huge shipyard Akers Mekaniske Verksted had been replaced by an upmarket consumption reservation and a few blocks of exorbitantly priced sea-view flats. Two of the three breweries had been transformed into colleges and business schools. Where, two decades ago, burly men were still lugging crates of lager and sorting empties, a moist roll-up resting in the corner of their mouth, one might find today men of a slighter build, wearing jeans and an open shirt, teaching groups of twentysomethings about cross-cultural communication. In Nydalen (New Valley), home to some of the oldest industry in Norway, all heavy industry had disappeared by the mid-1980s, to be replaced by enterprises characteristic of their time, the information age: a huge book-club corporation, Microsoft Norway, TV studios, a radio station and assorted consultancy and communication firms have taken over the bright, refurbished locales where thousands of workers spent their days in a recent past which suddenly seems very distant.

In the same period, global chains like McDonald's and 7-Eleven appeared for the first time, and by 2005, four major chains controlled more than ninety per cent of the retail trade in groceries. Leaving Oslo for a conference in Kuala Lumpur some years ago, the last thing I saw before entering the plane was a TGI Friday restaurant with a special offer on chicken. Disembarking in Malaysia, the first thing to meet my eyes upon leaving the plane, drowsy and nicotine-starved, was a TGI Friday restaurant with a special offer on chicken. The political reaction described by Holmes derives from a sense of flattening, where nothing has significance any more, as well as a dreadful feeling of superfluity.

What interests us in particular here, of course, is how Holmes brings his anthropological gaze and skills to bear on the topic. His concern is with the new right. To chart its compass and spread in the new Europe, he has carried out multi-sited ethnography of the kind advocated by George Marcus (1999), beginning in a north Italian valley and making his way to Strasbourg and Brussels, before ending up in London's East End.

Studying up tends to be more difficult than studying down. More is at stake for the rich and powerful than for those who 'have nothing to lose but their chains', they have less time on their hands, and they risk more by talking informally to strangers. It is an open question whether Holmes' fieldwork was a matter of studying up or studying down. He met, and had long conversations with, right-wing political leaders at all levels, from the small community council member to people like Jean-Marie Le Pen, the founder-leader of the Front National, and Richard Edmonds, the national organizer of the BNP (British National Party). The latter were powerful enough; the former appear mostly as working-class bigots seen through the eyes of a visitor from the middle class. Fast-capitalism, a global force if anything, is seen partly from the distance, partly through the eyes of some of its victims. Unlike a popular (and important!) book such as Naomi Klein's, which is known as *No Logo*, but which is actually called, somewhat less elegantly, *No Space, No Choice, No Jobs, No Logo: Taking Aim at the Brand Bullies* (Klein 1999), *Integral Europe* does not give the impression that the author has spoken to hundreds of disenfranchised workers or angry fascists. Rather, he oscillates between the macro and the micro, uses the macro for overviews and explanatory factors, and delves deeply into his chosen slivers of micro, which largely amount to the rationale behind the statements and the actions of dedicated right-wingers. As a result, we understand the logic of right-wing populism, or neo-fascism, much better than we did before. The recent 'Europeanization' of Le Pen's public persona is analysed and, for example, Holmes shows how Le Pen now speaks of 'cultural incommensurability' rather than using less polite terms, which he did in the past. There are also lengthy, very instructive excerpts from conversations between Holmes and other right-wing leaders in France and Britain, and if anything, the Frenchmen come across as more polished and suave in their style than their British counterparts, even if the politics are largely the same. Consider this statement from Roger Johnston, Le Pen's right-hand man: 'The growing immigration that comes from outside of Europe is a threat to our culture and our employment situation' (Holmes 2000: 87). Now compare it with this statement from Richard Edmonds: 'We use the term "racist" in a factual, what we would say a positive, sense. We describe a racist as someone who attempts to maintain Britain as racially white' (Holmes 2000: 116). Unlike the Front National, the BNP has apparently not discovered the 'new racism' yet, that which uses culture as a foil to mask colour prejudice.

Be this as it may, and tempting as it might be, we cannot lose ourselves in the rich fabric of Holmes' ethnography of the new right wing. Seen with the criteria of a more public, more engaged, less enclosed anthropology, Holmes does almost everything right. Unlike many others, he has actually spun a narrative, a story relating his own process of discovery. Beginning with integralists in Friuli, he unravels the chains and networks that connect neo-liberalism with neo-fascism by travelling through the epicentres of the European Union and ending, in the second part of the book, in the East End of London, before returning to Strasbourg, Le Pen and a couple of his speeches. The narrative is punctuated with analysis, especially in the first chapters, but there is no verbiage and no theorizing that doesn't lead anywhere. If there were any justice in the world, Holmes' book would be influential far beyond the confines of anthropology. If it were to become really successful in terms of influence, however, it would need to be even sharper in its central formulations on the connections between fast-capitalism, multiculturalism and neo-fascism, it would have to integrate the analytical framework more seamlessly, and most importantly, it would have to tell the story in a more straightforward and engaging way. *Integral Europe* is a great achievement, which speaks to many intellectual and political concerns, but it is less quotable than almost anything written by the aforementioned Berlin or Bauman. Holmes cannot be blamed: anthropologists just don't seem to take the craft of writing fluently and well seriously enough. Analysis, it seems, keeps getting in the way.

Ong's Diaspora Chinese

Another powerful anthropological monograph which addresses identity, or ident-ification, in the 'afterological' world (to use Sahlins', 1999, acid turn of phrase) is Aihwa Ong's award-winning book, *Flexible Citizenship*, about transnationalism and citizenship among Chinese (Ong 1999). Like Holmes' multi-sited ethnography, Ong's book covers a wider geographical area than most anthropology books. Again, like Holmes, Ong makes a number of arguments that feed directly into the general intellectual debate about 'clashes of civilizations', citizenship and identity, and class in an era of global politics.

If the North Atlantic working classes, core supporters for the new right-wing populist parties, have been victims of downward mobility, the Chinese diasporas seem to experience upward mobility wherever they settle. It has been estimated that in the Philippines, one per cent of the population, the Chinese minority that is, controls sixty per cent of the economy (Chua 2003). Riots in Indonesia have been directed against the market-dominant Chinese minority. Moreover, on the US west coast, in South-East Asia and from Moscow to Mauritius, locals are concerned with, and often worried about, the rise of a hugely successful expatriate Chinese business class. Ong's study shows that the facile view of globalization as 'Westernization' is misleading, that the boundaries of the nation-state are penetrated like a Swiss cheese, and that nations these days extend well beyond their physical territories. I can testify to this; during my first fieldwork in Mauritius, I was witness to an unprecedented economic transformation. The island, which had been dependent on sugar since the eighteenth century, was catapulted into the era of manufacturing in the space of a few years, and the Chinese Chamber of Commerce was instrumental in bringing it about, through its ability to attract investments from the Far East.

So Ong has a lot to write about. Money, power, movement, multiple strands of belonging, and of course kinship. The publisher's blurb made me slightly wary – the prose was cumbersome and seemed academically fashion-conscious – but my scepticism temporarily waned as I opened the book, which begins like this:

> On the eve of the return of Hong Kong from British to mainland Chinese rule, the city was abuzz with passport stories. A favourite one concerned mainland official Lu Ping, who presided over the transition. At a talk to Hong Kong business leaders (*taipans*), he fished a number of passports from his pockets to indicate he was fully aware that the Hong Kong elite has a weakness for foreign passports. (Ong 1999: 1)

The topic is thereby introduced in three short, powerful sentences. Chinese business elites abroad are suspected of being unfaithful to their nation-state, their ethnic identity as Chinese is not identical with their national identity, which might change according to circumstances, and the relationship with mainland China ('PRC', as it used to be known in US newspeak) is thus complicated. Like Holmes, but in a different style and using a very different kind of material, Ong questions the ability of the contemporary nation-state to contain people's loyalties, showing that they adapt pragmatically. The Chinese diasporas are connected with each other through kinship, language, culture and various kinds of economic networks. Most of them seem to have strong ethnic identities but a weak allegiance to China, and in this they differ from other transnational groups such as Sri Lankan Tamils, Turks or Pakistanis in Europe.

Ong sets out to make six arguments, she says in the introduction, all of them interesting for the enlightened public – but truth to tell, she is bound to lose at least half of the potential readership on the first ten pages, presuming anyone outside the circuits of Asia-Pacific studies and the anthropology of globalization were alerted to the book in the first place. The book does appear a bit bloated as you pick it up, in the manner of American novels, but it turns out to be an easy read, at least for those of us who are accustomed to reading academic prose. But many potential readers are not, and they will be lost. There is talk in the introduction of 'the transnational practices and imaginings of the nomadic subject', 'embeddedness in differently configured regimes of power' and so on. Now, as far as academic jargon goes, the usage is moderate here compared to many other books one could think of, but one is more attentive than usual to language in a book whose topic indicates that it deserves a wide readership. Who doesn't want to know about the spread of Chinese economic interests worldwide? And who isn't keen on understanding how the expatriate Chinese and their descendants feel about who they are and where they belong? I mean, if most of the Chinese in, say, Indonesia or the Philippines live in gated communities, avoid paying taxes and invest their surplus wherever it gives the highest yields, then one would take a slightly different view of the popular uprisings against them than one would if they were loyal citizens, philantropists to a man, committed not only to increasing their own fortunes but to developing their chosen country of residence as well.

Ong sheds much light on these questions, but she is at her best when she describes the salient features of a Chinese modernity, that has appropriated 'Asian values' (hard work, loyalty, family solidarity) and combined them with transnational ambitions. Unlike Holmes' book, *Flexible Citizenship* is not based on fieldwork, and there is little of the contextualized, experience-near ethnography here that one is used to in an anthropological monograph. Yet it is clear that the book could only have been written by an anthropologist trained in the last decades of the twentieth century, and one of its great merits consists in showing the rest of us that the methodology, as C. Wright Mills told us decades ago (Mills 1959), depends on the subject at hand. Careful not to essentialise 'Chinese culture', Ong nonetheless identifies and analyses cultural features governing the tightly integrated knots of diasporic Chinese, such as hierarchical, patrilineal kinship, the ethic of *guanxi* or interpersonal relations, and the ideology of racial exclusiveness that limits intermarriage. Ong also has interesting things to say about the sacrifices and trade-offs families have to make in order to become successful in competitive, often vaguely hostile environments. One teenager in southern California sarcastically refers to her father as 'the ATM machine' because, apparently, he provides money and little else. Ong also mentions couples who divorce because they never find an opportunity to spend time together. Flexibility is a key term in Ong's book, regrettably not defined; but it could be mentioned, staying with the spirit of her book, that a reed can be extremely flexible but sooner or later snaps in two.

Chua's Dominant Minorities

Chinese diasporas appear to be 'unmeltable ethnics' wherever they go. After a century, old Sino-Mauritian ladies in Port-Louis, Mauritius, remain more fluent in Hakka than in Creole. They nevertheless represent a kind of minority which is widespread in the non-North Atlantic world, and which is not necessarily Chinese, namely the kind described by Amy Chua (2003) as market-dominant minorities. If we are going to understand why it is that books such as Ong's never enter the discussions of the chattering classes, it might be an idea to take a look at Chua's *World on Fire*. Both books discuss aspects of globalization and identity politics, both focus on transnationalism, instability and elite groups, and both happen to be authored by female university professors of East Asian origin, working in the USA. Ong's book has been praised by anthropologists, while law professor Chua's was praised in *The Independent* and spent a long time on the *New York Times'* bestseller list.

Amy Chua's book is not necessarily better than Aihwa Ong's. Academic specialists are likely to find the latter more rewarding. Ong visibly struggles to find accurate words whereas Chua can be both glib and slick; Ong engages critically with received views of Chinese culture, globalization, liberalism and democracy, while Chua takes US world dominance for granted and prefers pithy conclusions to bewildering complexity. Chua's main argument can be summarized as the view that the conflict between liberal democracy and the economic dominance of ethnic elites leads to instability. The subtitle of the book puts it neatly: 'How Exporting Free Market Democracy Breeds Ethnic Hatred and Global Instability'.

There are three important, and I think relevant, differences between the books. First, Chua writes in a journalistic style. Instead of delving into intricate issues of terminology, she refers to the specialist literature. She revels in lucidity and has no time for Foucault. By contrast, Ong patiently tries out words to find a language which does justice to the complexities she describes (a kind of skill occasionally brought to dizzying heights in contemporary anthropology on both sides of the Atlantic).

Secondly, Chua's book is driven by narrative, while Ong's is driven by analysis. In Ong's *Flexible Citizenship*, short narratives introduce and illustrate; in Chua's *World on Fire*, the stories are the very engine and stuff of the book itself. The loftier and more generalizing statements at the beginning and the end are mere organizing principles for the stories she has to tell about the plight of market-dominant minorities in a world where the masses demand justice and equality.

Thirdly, Chua has a more inclusive way of communicating with her presumed readers. Addressing her middle-class American readership directly, she uses their language rather than knotty, cumbersome academic terms. Speaking from within a world of conventional middle-class sensibilities, she can have thousands of readers who are not only educated by her book, but who take pleasure in curling up with it.

Could *Flexible Citizenship* have been written in a similarly engaging and popular style without compromising its message? Well, yes and no. The analytic significance of a book does not depend on its use of fashionable jargon, but an argumentative book that does more than merely confirm views that the reader already held beforehand, has to offer some resistance. Chua, sympathetic to global capitalism, can hardly be said to do this, even if her postulated conflict between 'free' markets and democracy is controversial enough. However, no matter what one's agenda, even a critical intervention is executed more efficiently through striking, provocative narratives than through an insistence on arcane terminology and in-house rules of argument.

The fact may be that when anthropologists fail to reach the general intellectual public, it is because they have been taught to be more worried about the reactions from the people they eat lunch with than what people outside the university might think. As a result, they sometimes seem to write badly on purpose.

The reason I've treated Holmes and Ong in some detail is that their books are suggestive of the potentials of a public anthropology. Envisioned only slightly differently, written with a greater attention to style and an awareness of the existence of a jaded, but intelligent and engaged readership out there, they might have sold by the bucket-load.

And there are so many others that might have been mentioned, such a wealth of good, original, potentially important anthropological studies of identities in the contemporary world. Gerd Baumann's (1996) and Marie Gillespie's (1995) complementary studies of ethnicity in Southall (south-west London) demonstrate beyond a shadow of doubt that ethnicity in practice is something altogether less rigid and predictable than what one might expect from a reading of statistics or newspapers. The late Abner Cohen's study of the Notting Hill carnival (1993) is a brilliant exposé of hybridity; Karen Fog Olwig's work on transnationalism in the Caribbean and its diasporas (e.g. Olwig 2003) shows what a difficult concept 'home' has become, and this is only the first handful of studies that comes to mind. My argument is that with modest but determined effort, some of this work could have made a difference outside the subject and indeed outside the academy. Provided, of course, this is considered worthwhile.

Virulent Identity Politics and the Anthropologist

Another popular book that tries to make sense of identity politics, concentrating on its most virulent forms, is Benjamin Barber's *Jihad vs. McWorld*. Its instantly appealing (or discouraging, to some) title may have led many to assume that Barber's project resembles that of someone like Samuel Huntington, who has infamously argued that civilizational differences account for current conflicts; or that Barber simply believes that there is a deep chasm between 'the West and the Rest'. The book, written by a social scientist who cares about his readers, is the kind of book you'd be likely to find in a smallish airport bookshop almost anywhere in the world. First published in 1995, new prefaces have been added twice. First, in 2001, following the first British edition of the book, Barber takes the opportunity to reflect on the seeming lack of receptivity in the UK for his view (perhaps the British had found a 'middle way'?); then, in 2003, he reviews his thesis in the light of the 9/11 events and the ensuing 'war against terrorism'.

In fact, Barber's argument is more subtle, and more interesting, than the title suggests, and he is intellectually closer to sociologists like Robert Putnam (*Bowling Alone*) or George Ritzer (*The McDonaldization of Society*) than to apocalyptic prophets or simple-minded modernisers. The book – racy, witty and serious in its analysis – discusses the erosion of civil society: the increased dominance of the globalizing market, the author argues, renders citizens powerless and ultimately turns them into mere consumers. The loss of public spaces where citizens can interact in non-consuming modes leaves a nihilistic void which is exploited by irrational political groups. The loss of participatory democracy and the abdication of politics to the marketplace, in other words, is connected to the rise of identity politics, frequently based on religion or ethnic identity and, in the cases examined by Barber, using non-democratic and violent means. The book depicts a geopolitical order characterized by conflicts between territorial states and de-territorialized networks whose existence is possible because of the decline in participatory democracy and globalization in communications. It is not without its weaknesses – poverty is not addressed properly, nor is the fact that violent identity politics often arises in countries where civil society was weak in the first place, in other words that there need not be a direct connection between McWorld and Jihad (which, in Barber's usage, covers much more than Islamic holy war).

What is interesting here is not the strengths and weaknesses of *Jihad vs. McWorld*, but the fact that the book takes on a cluster of issues intensively studied by anthropologists, and has been commercially successful and politically influential. Clinton seems to have read it during his presidency, and the updated (post-9/11) edition can be purchased in reasonably well-stocked bookshops all over the world, in many languages including Farsi.

What might this book have looked like if it had been written by an anthropologist specializing in identity politics and globalization? Assuming, as a wild experiment of thought, that a social anthropologist was approached by a publisher who wanted someone to make sense of global tensions and conflicts in the period after the cold war?

To begin with, the book would have had to include greater empirical detail. Barber's examples often read like articles from the *Herald Tribune*, while an anthropologist would be likely to use material from his own fieldwork region extensively and recurrently, more cautious in his comparisons, and would need to question the category of 'the West' while presumably not abandoning it completely. Actually,

Barber's cavalier approach to empirical detail results in his book being littered with small but irritating errors. In just a few pages of the introduction, he misspells 'Pathan' as 'Panthan', describes Rwanda in the worst tabloid manner as 'slaughter-happy', and muses over the fact that reggae 'gets only a tiny percentage of MTV play time even in Latin markets' (p. 12) – well, one does not have to be a regional expert to know that reggae is a Jamaican invention. Unlike, say, Michael Ignatieff's or Timothy Garton Ash's books on Eastern Europe, this book carries a minimal imprint of the author's own experiences. There is scarcely any of what anthropologists would call first-hand empirical material.

Yet there are extremely good reasons for not merely turning one's nose up at this kind of book as 'not being anthropology' (of course it's not!). Granted that market fetishism is rampant and spreading globally, and there are good reasons for claiming that it is, and granted that the reactions to global capitalism and perceived US hegemony in the realms of geopolitics, mass culture and the world economy have some similarities in different places, there is every reason to expect anthropologists, 'peddlers in cultural difference', to have something to tell the public about this. To the extent that we haven't done so, we leave the discussion to others, which means, in practice, other social scientists and journalists.

An anthropological book about 'Jihad and McWorld' would have been finely attuned to nuance and local variation. Yet it would also have to concede that certain ideologies and cultural identities currently take on a transnational character, and that discrete events are interconnected. I drafted this section in early autumn 2004, the aftermath of the hostage drama in Bislan, North Ossetia, which coincided with the kidnapping of more than twenty NGO workers in Darfur, the abduction of two Frenchmen and the killing of twelve Nepalese in Iraq, and several suicide bombings in Israel. Some of the hostage-takers in Bislan were said to have been Arabs. Osama bin Laden, who has also fought Russians in Chechnya, had a close relationship with the regime in Sudan for years. The Iraqi insurgency is partly motivated by religion, partly by less specific resentment towards the occupying forces. Such connections, documented or rumoured, would have to be elaborated upon by an anthropologist, notwithstanding many anthropologists' current reluctance to look beyond their own region of specialization.

But on the whole, an anthropologist would have gone deeper into each example. The result may have become less convincing than Barber in describing global uniformities, but instead such a book would have delved into local specificities of kinds usually ignored. It would show that although the forces leading to identity politics in all its forms – democratic and anti-democratic, from above and from below – are truly global in scope and reach, any explanation or even description which does not see globalization through the lens of local meanings and struggles, is inadequate. As Aihwa Ong has shown, there is something peculiar to Chinese diasporas, and Chinese politics of identity does not resemble Islamic politics of identity except in the most general way.

Such a book might profit from employing the 'whodunit' structure of the suspense novel, or the 'riddle' format. According to the received wisdom, Tutsis and Hutus are different tribes with different cultures, and their mutual animosities are partly ancient, partly created by the Belgians. An anthropologist, with or without first-hand experience of Rwanda and Burundi, would be likely to question the very categories of Tutsi and Hutu, indicating the ambiguities and mobility across the ethnic boundary, demonstrating cultural similarities (language, religion, way of life), and would almost certainly show how Hutu and Tutsi became reified as statistical census categories in fairly recent times. Hopefully, this anthropologist would not baulk at objective data, but would concede that the conflicts in the region are connected to land and water shortages caused by a trebling of the population in a little more than a generation. Thus the 'atavistic tribal war' might be translated into a desperate struggle over scarce resources where alignments were based on almost random, but state-sanctioned, 'ethnic' distinctions.

Unlike most books on the subject, the popular anthropological book about virulent identity politics would show that the term 'ethnic conflict' is an empty vessel, since people do not have conflicts over ethnicity. Ethnic identity or religion instead functions as a symbolic focus, a means of mobilization and a pretext for transgressing rules and norms. After stating something to this effect, our anthropologist would need to leave his own fieldwork and compare cases such as Hindu nationalism, the European extreme right, Palestinian resistance and so on, using several pages to describe each of them and concluding that the globalized struggles involving market liberalism and collective identities are, at the end of the day, always local.

This book would also have to go more deeply into the social and psychological foundations of identification than what is common. How, for example, can intimacy, trust and reciprocity be transformed into fundamentalist attitudes, and how do such relationships, crucial in human lives, develop in the first place? How can loyalty towards others turn into hatred and resentment of outsiders? And – this is one of anthropology's classic tours de force – how does a person's identification shift from situation to situation? Why do so many tightly organized, politically potent groups have religious and ethnic labels? A popular anthropological book on antagonistic identity politics would have to come clean on questions regarding human nature. Since humans are social and depend on trust for their psychological well-being, perceived betrayals of our webs of trust are perceived as grave threats to our very existence. Relationships of trust are not merely biological, however, but depend on metaphoric and symbolic extensions of primary relationships. If my primary attachment to my family and intimates is extended metaphorically to include fellow citizens, fellow believers or something similar, then I would react in a personal and existentially urgent way whenever someone threatens such imagined communities.

Thus an anthropology of contemporary identity politics has to ask where particular identities come from, not just historically, but in our universal human experience – and how it can be that they are expressed so variously.

Actually, the scenario described a few paragraphs ago is not unthinkable; a very similar one unfolded some years ago in Oslo. In February 1995, following a public intervention on my part in connection with the Rushdie Affair, I was contacted by a publisher who asked me to write a book about 'the West and Islam'. I had reacted against the cocksure and monolithic human rights fundamentalism that dominated the debate in Scandinavia, and had noticed (although I didn't say it publicly) that some of the most confident defenders of universal freedom of speech had been similarly confident Maoists a decade or two earlier. As if social context and historical experiences had nothing to do with attitudes to freedom of speech! My view was that if we are going to be cultural imperialists, and I suppose we are, then let us at least be knowledgeable, respectful and open-minded cultural imperialists.

Although I felt strongly about these issues, I reacted to the publisher's suggestions with some hesitation. I have never done fieldwork in a predominantly Muslim country and was not keen to pose as an expert in geopolitics. In the end, that is to say after a couple of days, I nonetheless accepted the commission and the book was published at the end of the year with the title *Det Nye Fiendebildet* [The New Enemy Image]. A new, updated and expanded edition called *Bak Fiendebildet* [Behind the Enemy Image], (Eriksen 2001a) was published a few months after 9/11. The book set forth to explain how 'the West' and 'Islam' are passing historical constructions that may nevertheless become self-fulfilling prophecies. Like many others, I criticised Samuel Huntington for his simplistic beliefs in 'civilizational faultlines' – based on ideas about culture popular in the late Victorian era – and likewise criticized another influential conservative intellectual, Francis Fukuyama, for believing that the American way was the only game worth playing in the global village. I threw in a bit of post-colonial theory, many stories about humiliation experienced by immigrants, a critical appraisal of the Rushdie Affair, and – in the second edition – a bit about the comparative advantages of scattered networks as opposed to territorial power, as well as some musings about political Islam as a global family of counter-cultural movements, or perhaps alternative modernities. The main argument was that recognition and, conversely, the ability to listen were some of the scarcest resources in the contemporary world.

The book, short and modest in its ambitions, was not an anthropology book (it contained hardly any original ethnography, and had few references to other anthropologists), but I couldn't have written it without being an anthropologist. It rejected universalizing narratives about 'the direction of world history' and insisted on the primacy of the local, as well as stressing the knotty and intricate webs of connectedness that make reductionist statements about this or that group being 'chiefly Muslim' patently ludicrous. The very same people who were considered 'guest workers' in the 1970s became 'Pakistanis' and 'Turks' a decade later, before becoming 'Muslims' in the 1990s. Nobody asked them how they would prefer to identify themselves.

A main difficulty in writing this kind of text, which is politically engaged at the same time as it tries not to compromise the anthropological way of thinking, consists in negotiating the line between cultural relativism and political commitment – incidentally the very contradiction identified in the liberal tradition by John Gray in his *Two Faces of Liberalism* (Gray 2000). A working solution is often to be found in perspectivism and contextualism. Or, to put it differently: Only an idiot would believe that his form of government, and his political ideas, would arise *sui generis* anywhere in the world, if one just got rid of the bad guys. So local context cannot be ignored. Moreover, nobody can deny that world history looks different from Hanoi than it does from London. So what you see depends not just on what you are looking at or even what you are looking through, but also where you are looking from. All of this is plain common sense to an anthropologist, but not necessarily to everybody else.

There is, naturally, a lot more that anthropologists might want to say about identity politics. The role of the State in simplifying and freezing categories of race, ethnicity and religion has been studied by many in illuminating ways. The gap between official and popular perceptions has likewise been documented, and the fiction of 'irreconcilable cultural differences' has been exposed often enough. But these things need to be said again and again, and pointing out that Leach said this forty years ago, or for that matter Boas eighty years ago, as some of us occasionally do, can sometimes function as an excuse for laziness and smug detachment.

Making the Foreign Familiar

Anthropologists excel in communicating the experiences of others to people who share their own experiences and representations. They tend to be less skilled when it comes to drawing on the experiences of their outside readership. At this point, narrative skills become relevant. As every schoolgirl knows (or at least every anthropology undergraduate), the threshold for empathy is called identification. The foreign needs to be made familiar, either by describing the foreigners as if they were familiar or by showing how their lives are similar to, and connected to, ours. In the context of world politics, this is absolutely crucial, and few are in a better position to do the job than anthropologists.

There is a genre of Norwegian journalism which one might call 'No Norwegians were harmed'. It is a version of the old British story from the days before the Chunnel, when stormy weather in the North Sea prevented ferries from crossing. The apocryphal British newspaper headline read: 'Bad weather in the North Sea: the Continent isolated'.

Whenever disaster strikes – earthquakes, insurgencies, wars – one of the first tasks of the press consists in finding out whether any of our nationals were in the region, and their present whereabouts. This is understandable and probably defensible; the problem arises when there is a systematic asymmetry in the coverage of different kinds of foreigners' deaths. As a European NGO worker in Sudan exclaimed during the Darfur famine: These children's mistake consisted in not having made their way to the World Trade Center! As everyone knows, three thousand middle-class professionals from the USA have an immensely higher value than a few hundred thousand unknown African illiterates. Since this fact makes claims about universal humanism sound hollow, anthropologists (and others) may now and then take the time to remind their compatriots why it is that in fact Afghan lives are just as valuable as the lives next door, but that our media rarely allow us to discover this.

Anthropologists are too rarely able to connect with their public spheres in times of crisis. To take some of the most publicized conflicts of the 1990s, none of the most influential texts about Bosnia, Sri Lanka, Somalia or Rwanda were written by anthropologists. Alex de Waal's incisive and penetrating writings in various formats and addressing a variety of audiences notwithstanding, anthropologists have been slow to react efficiently to crises. De Waal, a founder of the small but influential NGO African Rights, published a shocking book about famine in Darfur as early as 1989, and his writings sparkle with engagement and determination, like the work of a few others who ply the waters between academic work and advocacy, such as David Maybury-Lewis, another anthropologist who has turned himself into an influential activist and popularizer.

Yet the anthropologists are rarely far away when war or famine breaks out. They have often been eyewitnesses and even if they haven't been, they are among the most knowledgeable people, obvious specialists to consult about. say, the intricacies of local-level politics in Afghanistan, the ultimate causes of the genocide in Rwanda and the significance of ethnicity in the former Yugoslavia. Anthropologists have written incisively about these issues – some, such as Liisa Malkki's (1995) book about Rwanda, and Tone Bringa's (1996) book about Bosnia are chilling documents, well documented and morally engaged. But of course, they were published after the dust had settled, and were presumably read chiefly by regional specialists apart from other anthropologists.

In previous chapters I have argued that speed is a factor in determining whether or not one is able to make an impact through the media, and it is evidently the case here too. The Swedish anthropologist Staffan Löfving, himself an ex-journalist, reflects on the differences in temporality between anthropology and journalism: 'Writing slowly about fast changes constitutes a paradox in anthropology. The paradox of journalism consists in writing quickly and sometimes simplistically about complex changes' (Löfving 2004: 139).

Confronting the same paradox, Hannerz (2004a: 16f.) humorously speculates on the possibility of 'parachute anthropology', if highly competent teams of anthropologists scattered around our university departments were equipped and ready to leave instantly for the field – tent and malaria pills waiting in an office corner – like firefighters, if something urgent came up. Presumably this team of urgent anthropologists should also be prepared to write up their findings really fast. Hannerz, who has done fieldwork on foreign correspondents in recent years (Hannerz 2003), nevertheless notes that it is not just the anthropologists who chase the big events in the 'already cold' footprints of journalists. After all, there are Asia correspondents based in Hong Kong who are expected to report authoritatively on events in Jordan.

The media sphere's demands for speed cannot be met by fieldwork-based anthropology. It necessarily takes longer to analyse and present the data than a newspaper or commercial publisher can accept. However, it is far from impossible to write engaging and important work based on knowledge one already possesses, or which can quickly be accessed through the available professional literature. It is easy to think of examples of serious, well researched, successful books and other kinds of interventions addressing contemporary political issues, which may have made a difference in the political arena itself. Some are written by journalists like Thomas Friedman (*The Lexus and the Olive Tree*, 1999) or Robert Kaplan (*The Ends of the Earth*, 1997), or by academics who have reinvented themselves as journalists (or the other way around), like Timothy Garton Ash, Fred Halliday and Michael Ignatieff. Yet others, like Noam Chomsky and the late Edward Said, use their professorial authority to make statements pertaining to areas where they are not specialists in an academic sense.

It is this latter category that constitutes the public intellectual proper. Richard Dawkins, voted Britain's #1 public intellectual, rarely leaves biology in his writings, but he has recently been writing about race and politics (2004) – an area where many would argue that anthropologists are the most knowledgeable academics – and he made a comment about religion immediately after 11 September 2001. Compared to many other public intellectuals, Dawkins is careful to set topical limits for his engagements, but anthropologists rarely venture even as far as he does from their area of expertise. Every day, we seem to confirm the common saying that the contemporary academic knows more and more about less and less.

It is true that the rigours of carrying out fieldwork, writing up and establishing authority within social and cultural anthropology usually imply intense concentration on a limited set of questions, very often asked in relation to an intensively studied and compact empirical material. I think most practising anthropologists contribute to the fragmentation of the discipline, often *malgré eux*, in their teaching of these ideals. In fact, during supervision of an MA student today, I was confronted with her anxiety about writing in 'too general a mode' about Turkey between West and East. After all, the fieldwork had zoomed in on middle-class Istanbul dwellers in their twenties and their personal ways of dealing with the tensions between Western modernity and Islam. I told her that a short chapter on Turkish history was entirely in order, remarking on the area's place in ancient philosophy, the waves of settlement from the east, the multinational character of the Ottoman empire, the authoritarian secularism of Kemal Atatürk and the contemporary, troubled relationship with the EU on the one hand and Islam on the other. But, she objected, this is supposed to be anthropology, not history or political science. Well, I responded, the chapter we're discussing now provides context, and you move on from there to the real thing – your own field material – as quickly as possible.

This kind of comment, passed often enough in anthropology departments worldwide, gives the students the impression that there exists a universal hierarchy of knowledge, with ethnography on top. Accordingly, the hubris of social and cultural anthropology traditionally consists in the idea that it was possible, as William Blake famously put it in his 'Auguries of Innocence',

> To see the world in a grain of sand
> And a heaven in a wild flower,
> Hold infinity in the palm of your hand,
> And eternity in an hour.

However, following the end of modernism (Ardener 1985), that is the general loss of faith in universal patterns, the imperial ambitions of anthropologists have waned, and what is left is mere ethnography – the grain of sand without the world, not to mention eternity. To compensate for this loss, many anthropologists have discovered history as an alternative source for developing a somewhat larger tapestry than the one offered by ethnography, but systematic comparison – once the hallmark of anthropology – is nowadays taught half-heartedly and only practised occasionally.

Adding this to comments made previously about the causes of anthropology's weak position in the public sphere, we begin to understand why the books and articles enlightening the general public about the state of the world are hardly ever written by anthropologists. Their world simply fails to connect with ours. Whenever there is a global or regional crisis, thousands of anthropologists, including those who are familiar with the region in question as well as others, are trying very hard to avoid coming to terms with it. Which is to say, they analyse and criticize a lot amongst themselves, some of them write excellent academic articles about the situation at hand – and, in all fairness, they sometimes surface in the media or in mainstream publications. But this is the exception rather than the rule. Occasionally, the revealing monograph is published, but always after the fact. During the break-up and ensuing wars of Yugoslavia, the Anglophone writers explaining and trying to influence opinion about the conflict in lengthy articles, essays and books, were all non-anthropologists (although, in all fairness, Tone Bringa's brilliant film *We Have Always Been Neighbours* did make an impact after the end of the war). The anthropologists discussed among themselves. In connection with the Vietnam War, anthropologists seem to have been more concerned with the possible misuse of their ethnographies (by the USA) than with active intervention (Salemink 2003).

Moreover, as Patrick Wilken (1994) has showed, anthropologists were virtually absent from the public eye during and after the first Gulf War. This is unsettling, as anthropologists specializing in the region possessed knowledge about local circumstances, which might have shifted public opinion about the legitimacy of both the Gulf War and future wars. In fact, by virtue of their close-up view of social life, anthropologists can tell troubling truths about *any* war, by giving a face and a voice to the victims and showing the visceral and gruesome reality of violence to audiences accustomed to sanitized TV violence, real or virtual.

All is not hopeless. A handful of media comments by American anthropologists following the 9/11 attack (see González 2004) demonstrate that anthropologists are able and sometimes willing to address urgent political questions outside their field of specialization, and that they are perfectly capable of adding their ethnography-coloured drop of complexity to the palette of ideas that makes up the public sphere, relinquishing detailed analysis temporarily in order to tell stories from the wide world instead.

Roberto Gonzàlez's edited book has the promising title *Anthropologists in the Public Sphere* and contains fifty-two chapters, all of them written by academic anthropologists addressing public issues – race, insurgencies and armed conflicts, American hegemony and the recent 'war on terror'. Aimed largely at an American student readership, the collection confines itself to American media. It is also somewhat limited in scope given its title; there are lots of other subject areas where anthropologists can have an impact as public intellectuals, such as development, indigenous issues, simplistic evolutionary tales, the vicissitudes of identification, consumption and modern living in general. González's book aims to show that anthropologists can function as critical intellectuals by speaking up against power, and that in doing so – not as academics, but as citizens – they draw on their professional knowledge and insights.

In spite of its excellent intentions, González's book inadvertently confirms that anthropologists tend to be far away from the mainstream discourse of their society even when there is a critical situation somewhere. The book covers eighty years of public interventions by American anthropologists, largely in the press, and it runs to about 250 pages, editorial introductions included. It includes about the same amount of text as a good journalist might churn out in a couple of months. Of course, the book does not include everything, but nowhere does the editor signal that he has had difficulties in making his selection. Moreover, many of the articles are specialist contributions – they rectify errors and add depth and perspective – rather than being interventions by engaged generalizts. As noted earlier, William O. Beeman (represented with three entries) seems to be the only American anthropologist who writes regularly for the press. In tiny Norway, by contrast, anthropologists are so used to handling the media that they often use the press to argue against each other.

The book is nonetheless very useful, ranging as it does from Margaret Mead on war to David Price, Laura Nader and Hugh Gusterson on academic freedom. Some of them might have been developed into articles for magazines or books for more long-term impact. All texts suggest that 'contextual, historical knowledge about other cultures' (González 2004: 16) makes terms like 'collateral damage' difficult to stomach and the prison camp in Guantanamo Bay impossible to tolerate by anyone with a humanist outlook.

At the end of his epilogue on anthropology and US world dominance, González quotes 'one anthropologist' at length without revealing the name. This person says:

> I am aware that this discussion is unconventional anthropology, but these are un-conventional times. We are all involved in unconventional and portentous military and political events... These events have worldwide consequences. It is time that we accepted some unconventional responsibilities for our acts, be they acts of commission or of omission. (In Gonzàlez 2004: 266)

It appears, then, that a concerned colleague is making a statement about the new era of American geopolitics here, the 'with us or with the terrorists' logic of the so-called war on terror. The endnote reference reveals, surprisingly, that the origin of the quotation is a 1968 article by Gerald Berreman, quoted in the first chapter of this book and questioning the role of anthropologists in conflicts such as the Vietnam War. If anything, Berreman's statement indirectly tells us that 'conventional times' are unlikely to return and that there are limits to complacency when we live in the eye of a whirlwind. Ours are the stories that hardly anybody else bothers about, and they need to be told in a variety of formats – the film, the newspaper article, the magazine article, the page-turner, the learned article or monograph.

–6–

Altercentric Writing

For a while in the mid-1990s, the philosopher Denis Dutton ran an annual bad writing contest, inviting readers of his journal *Philosophy and Literature* to submit their favourite snippets. Apart from an honourable mention for Stephen Tyler in the third contest, no anthropologists were on Dutton's shortlists, which were dominated by writers working in the border area between literary studies, cultural studies and philosophy. Partly this was because the journal dealt with exactly this intersection, but it is also probably true that the writing encountered in this area is often much more stilted, impenetrable and tending towards the vacuous than in most other fields, academic or non-academic. Few anthropologists are likely to even contemplate writing sentences like the following:

> The move from a structuralist account in which capital is understood to structure social relations in relatively homologous ways to a view of hegemony in which power relations are subject to repetition, convergence, and rearticulation brought the question of temporality into the thinking of structure, and marked a shift from a form of Althusserian theory that takes structural totalities as theoretical objects to one in which the insights into the contingent possibility of structure inaugurate a renewed conception of hegemony as bound up with the contingent sites and strategies of the rearticulation of power.

Not a sentence to be read aloud by people with limited lung capacity, this quotation from Judith Butler (1st prize, bad writing contest 1998) cannot easily be translated into lucid prose, simply because it is hard to see what it is about. Even the most 'difficult' anthropologists would be unlikely to write in this kind of style. Whenever they write badly, it tends to be a result of carelessness or laziness rather than attempts to seem profound and complex. And quite often, writing that seems bad is actually complex and conscientious, offering resistance when necessary instead of glib smoothness. Take, for example, this paragraph by Marilyn Strathern, who is often (and to my mind unfairly) accused of deliberately writing impenetrable prose:

> Think of a culture where bodily experiences are not hidden away to be encountered as secret knowledge that resists social control, but where they are the subject of overt attention for men as well as women. And a culture which does not hypostatise 'the body' as such, for the body is not an external yet possessed presence, and integrated whole, but where on the contrary body imagery suggests social disjunction as well as conjunction.

> Where, indeed, every body is a composite of different identities; where bodies do not belong to persons but are composed of the relations of which a person is composed. Finally, then, a culture where partibility or fragmentation of persons/bodies is not the unintended result but as much as (*sic*) explicit *aim* of people's actions as is their unity. (Strathern 1992:76)

This is vintage Strathern, reflecting on kinship and relatedness, the boundaries of the person and the possibilities of imagining persons as being made up of their relationships to others. The language is knotty and spiky, offering solid resistance against any attempt to be read superficially. One may like or dislike her style, but it is hard to argue that it is unnecessarily complicated, or that she hides in a difficult language because she has little to say. As in most of Strathern's writings, there are few arcane or technical terms. The complexity lies in the *ideas*. Building on feminist theory and the contrast between Melanesian and British kinship (she has done fieldwork on both), she argues that persons may perfectly well be seen not as autonomous entities, but rather as the sum total of their relationship to others. The writing could nonetheless have been more elegant. For example, she might have put it like this:

> Think of a culture where bodily experiences are not hidden away and subjected to shame and secrecy. Instead, they are openly viewed and discussed by both men and women. There, 'the body' would not be seen as an entity in itself, but rather as an integrated part of the social surroundings. In fact, every body would be composed of different identities and relationships. Also, in this culture, the fragmentation of the person would not be seen as a problem, but indeed as a normal aspect of what it means to be human.

Yet, the style is not a major problem here. On the contrary, Strathern is making herself perfectly understood to her intended readership, that is anthropologists and other academics interested in kinship and relatedness. A book about the same topic ought to be written for a general audience, and preferably by an anthropologist, but there is no pressing reason why Strathern should do it herself. Moreover, refusing to acknowledge that texts sometimes have to offer resistance, especially if they are trying to say something new, would be blatant populism. Sometimes, ideas are compromised, or flattened, if they are translated into a nondescript middle-class prose. It can be necessary to be difficult if you have difficult things to say.

The point that I'm getting to, which is the message of this chapter, is that whether one's intended readership is a hundred or a hundred thousand, a writer should think very hard about who they might be. Sometimes difficult writing has to make for difficult reading. Aristotle can be excruciatingly difficult to read, even if academic jargon had yet to be invented when he wrote. But a writer has an obligation towards his or her audience. Some try to impress their readers, others try to intimidate them. Some appear as teachers, others as friends. Some readers want to be impressed, especially when young, and are easy victims for the peacocks of academia unless they are lucky enough to stumble across the truly profound (with limited experience, it can be difficult to see the difference); others simply want to be taught, and yet others enjoy having some knowledgeable person to discuss with.

In his discussion of successful popularization in anthropology, Sutton (1991) is especially concerned with the question of readership. Scrutinizing the strategies employed by Marvin Harris, Wade Davis and Ashley Montagu, he concludes that they differ a great deal from one another, but in all cases, 'their writing is directly concerned with the context of its reception' (Sutton 1991: 100). Harris asks riddles (although, as Marshall Sahlins once remarked, the answer is always protein). Davis applies a storytelling mode and appeals, like a novelist, to the shared world inhabited by both the reader and himself. Montagu, finally, initiates a kind of dialogic relation-ship with the reader in Sutton's view, actively asking for the reader's reactions and arguing that the ideas he presents ought to make a difference to the reader's life.

Anthropologists are not trained to be eloquent. Unlike the historians, anthropo-logists are not taught, or even encouraged, to write well. On the whole, non-initiates confronted with typical anthropological writing are likely to agree with Pratt (1986: 33) who wonders, 'how … could such interesting people doing such interesting things produce such dull books?' Now, they are sometimes able to escape from dull-ness. Many anthropologists are in fact excellent writers, but it is almost as if they try to conceal it in order to conform to the standards of style set by their peers.

That many anthropologists are perfectly capable of writing well, is regularly demonstrated in the pages of a magazine such as *Anthropology Today*. In fact, many of the contributions to *AT* are so good, so well written and interesting for a general readership, that one can only lament the fact that this magazine published by the Royal Anthropological Institute, a body committed to the popularization of anthropology, is only being distributed to anthropologists. As usual, anthropologists are rather good at talking to each other, but don't seem to worry too much about the rest of the world. As a matter of fact, many of the most respected anthropologists are able to write engagingly and well. Geertz is the first name that comes to mind; but Marshall Sahlins also sparkles with wit and intelligent puns as a speaker at public functions (Sahlins 1993); and both Mary Douglas and Lévi-Strauss can be damn fine writers when they set their mind to it. Just to mention a few of the biggest names.

What counts as effective writing has changed, in anthropology as elsewhere, since the early twentieth century. In Malinowski's time, the anthropologist was expected to be an omniscient observer offering not only ethnographic detail but also a general overview to his motley readership. Thus Malinowski introducing the Trobrianders:

The coastal populations of the South Sea Islands, with very few exceptions, are, or were before their extinction, expert navigators and traders. Several of them had evolved excellent types of large sea-going canoes, and used to embark in them on distant trade expeditions or raids of war and conquest. The Papuo-Melanesians, who inhabit the coast and the outlying islands of New Guinea, are no exception to this rule. (Malinowski 1984 [1922]: 1).

Today, this way of introducing the field would appear preposterous and pompous. It is now paramount that the anthropologist keeps her ears near the ground, and far from being absent or making cameo appearances in the text, she can often be a character, a positioned agent, herself; indeed, contemporary ethnographic authority relies to a great extent on subjective 'I-witnessing'. Consider this passage at the beginning of an article by Philippe Bourgois:

> I did not run fast enough out of the door of the video arcade crackhouse to avoid hearing the lookout's baseball bat thud twice against a customer's skull. I had misjudged the harsh words. Caesar, the lookout, had been exchanging with a drug-intoxicated customer to be the aggressive but ultimately playful posturing that is characteristic of much male interaction on the street. (Bourgois 2002: 15)

These words are saturated with speed, drama and violence, and introduce the ethnographer as a slightly anxious character who is forced to deal with the unpredictability of a patently dangerous neighbourhood. Bourgois's text about cocaine and gang crime in New York takes us a long way from Malinowski's serene tableau from the South Seas, but both count as efficient openings in my book: they take the reader by the hand (or by the lapels) immediately, at the outset of the text, and guide him into a cultural universe which presumably has little in common with the place where he carries out his everyday affairs. Yet, although both introductory paragraphs arguably succeed in catching the attention of the reader, neither of them is particularly well written. Malinowski's text is dry and lexicographical; Bourgois's text lacks rhythm and musicality, and its first and last sentences contain too many clumsily clustered words to read smoothly. If these introductions still work for non-professional readers, and they do, it is because of their tantalizing content. In Bourgois, there is speed and violence; in Malinowski, there is cultural difference and the lure of the South Seas.

Far too often, however, the excitement of an anthropological text stops on the title page; anthropological monographs surprisingly often have beautiful poetic titles which betray their tedious (if often important) contents. It may be that a bid for recognition as 'real science' in the mid-twentieth century is partly to blame, but whatever the case may be, it is a fact that anthropologists do not value good writing as highly as they ought to. I, for one, have told postgraduate students more than a few times that it doesn't matter if their work is not particularly well written or dramatic in its build-up, as long as it is lucid, linear and develops cumulatively. However, a consequence of this attitude may be that when anthropologists one day wish to to write for people other than members of their own profession, they discover that they have lost the language that would have enabled them to reach out.

Malinowski was aware that bad writing could alienate professional anthropology from its potential readership, and clumsily admitted, in the first chapter of *Argonauts*:

Needless to add ... the scientific field-work is far above even the best amateur produc-
tions. There is, however, one point in which the latter often excel. This is, in the
presentation of intimate touches of native life, in bringing home to us these aspects of it
with which one is made familiar only through being in close contact with the natives, one
way or the other, for a long period of time. (Malinowski 1984 [1922]: 17)

Yet for Malinowski this problem was most pronounced in quantitative survey work
entailing superficial work on large samples, because it could be overcome in vivid
ethnographic description based on long-term participant observation. It is nevertheless
debatable to what extent he, or the majority of his successors, demonstrated that it
was in fact possible to combine scientific rigour with good narrative writing. It can
be argued that they chose an audience of the already converted. As I search the
anthropological literature, canonical or not, for good storylines developed in vivid,
sparkling language, the anecdote about the anthropologist and the historian keeps
haunting me: The anthropologist dries out the living river, while the historian brings
water to the dry riverbed. It may be true that anthropologists care no less for their
readers than other writers do, but they are at their most effective when addressing
readers who are already hooked. The historians, by contrast, have a centuries-old
tradition of responsibility for enlightening the people. It is not their sole *raison
d'être*, but writing for non-specialists has always been a respectable activity among
historians, while anthropologists have spent a good part of the twentieth century
turning their noses up at the 'rustling-of-the-wind-in-the-palm-trees' style of writing
that could have been one way of giving the subject a broader impact.

In Search of Zombis

The rare publishing successes of anthropology can always teach us something
about the craft of writing, the many forms of translation – Paul Feyerabend once
said that the best translation of a book by Dostoyevsky might be one by Dickens
– and, occasionally, the temptations of literary populism. Wade Davis's remarkably
successful *The Serpent and the Rainbow* (Davis 1985) represents one kind of popular
anthropology at its very best, and tells us more about the first two than the third.
Perhaps the immediacy and fluidity of this book about *voudun*, the zombi puzzle
and Haitian peasant society is connected to the fact that it was written quickly. Davis
stepped off the plane in Port-au-Prince in April 1982; three years later, the book was
out. Considering that this was his first book, as well as the conventionally slow pace
of academic writing, not to mention the often gruelling process of refereeing and
actual publishing of academic texts, the speed is almost miraculous – even more so
as the book is really well crafted. *The Serpent and the Rainbow* is a rare example
of an anthropology book from recent decades which has enjoyed popular success as
well as respectful nods from fellow academics.

What can the rest of us learn from a book like this? For one thing, the book defines its problem – what lies at the heart of the alleged phenomenon of Haitian zombis – succinctly and without any unnecessary elaboration. For another, it does not burden the reader with intimidating references to arcane theory and in-crowd texts. (Now, I would in fact argue that some popular anthropology books should in fact do just this, minus the intimidation, but it is unnecessary in a book that is mainly ethnographic.) And of course, Davis was lucky enough to have a story to tell which was bound to catch the interest of many.

If told the right way, that is. Through his book, Davis comes across first and foremost as an adventurer and a storyteller, and almost incidentally as an academic. It could make the rest of us think that maybe we have this in ourselves too, but – alas – we never cared to look.

The story is told in the right manner, but in meandering and idiosyncratic ways. Davis enjoys telling stories, and sometimes his comparative imagination, stretched by snippets of undergraduate lore and recent swotting for exams, carries him far from Haiti – to instances of poisoning in the Russian court, to a story about an anthropologist among the Yaqui of Mexico and so on. He even has the nerve to include, in the first chapters of the book, a narrative from his own first field experience in the Amazon. All this is easily forgiven by the sympathetic reader, who is more likely than not to be a non-anthropologist. Davis takes visible joy from telling stories and is unafraid of his readers. Far from making them feel inadequate or awed, Davis tells jokes, often of a slapstick kind, at his own expense, and carries his learning lightly. But he is far from alien to the lure of the exotic and grotesque. Dealing with a particularly nasty ordeal in West Africa as a precursor to *voudun*, he describes the court hearing like this:

> If the accused was lucky enough to vomit and regurgitate the poison, he was judged innocent and allowed to depart unharmed. If he did not vomit, yet managed to reach the line, he was also deemed innocent, and quickly given a concoction of excrement mixed with water which had been used to wash the external genitalia of a female. (Davis 1985: 42)

The Serpent and the Rainbow is difficult to place in one of the categories listed in my first chapter. It is a single-person narrative where the reader follows the anthropologist on his path of discovery, and as such, it can almost be read as a *Bildungsroman*. At the outset, Davis is an unfocused student with wavering motivation, idly drinking coffee with a fellow student; towards the end, he metamorphoses into an accomplished ethnobotanist with a Real Discovery to show for himself.

But the book is also an anthropological whodunit, or riddle, where the mysteries of Haitian *voudon* religion and, in particular, the strange phenomenon of the zombi form the centrepiece. Davis does indeed encounter zombis eventually, and he identifies the poison causing their uncanny condition as 'living dead'. However, like any good suspense writer, when the mystery finally seems to have been unravelled, he takes the plot to a new level and delves into the deep cultural context of Haitian beliefs and ritual practices. He documents the informal power wielded by the Tonton Macoutes and the secret societies administering not only poison but various other forms of sanctions as well, and discusses the origins of Haitian peasant culture in Nigerian societies and plantation slavery. By now, the reader is likely to be so engrossed by the people of Haiti and charmed by their ethnographer that she is prepared to accept as much contextual complexity as it takes to get to the bottom of *voudun*. As a reward, the reader is given to understand that it does not arise *sui generis* but is connected to state violence and local power struggles.

In the main sections of the book, Davis enlivens his text with dialogue – real, racy dialogue that is, not lengthy informants' statements – and frank characterizations of individuals of a kind that most anthropologists would, for better or worse, shy away from. The cast of persons featured in the book, moreover, would be worthy of a Graham Greene novel – in fact, the characters Davis describes so vividly are even more varied and exciting than the people inhabiting Greene's Haitian novel, *The Comedians*. On the opening pages of Davis's story, we meet the legendary ethnobotanist Richard Evans Schultes, who had once taken a semester's leave to collect plants in the Amazon and subsequently disappeared into the forest for eight years. We also meet, on the opening pages, a cast of eccentric, but highly accomplished scientists giving fatherly advice, switching between sphinx-like and warning modes, to Davis on the eve of his departure. The Haitians are also painted with a literary brush, and come across as diverse, fascinating personalities. Our first encounter with the important local expert Max Beauvoir reads like this:

> There, among a dusty collection of amulets and African art, Max Beauvoir awaited me. He was immediately impressive – tall, debonair in dress and manner, and handsome. Fluent in several languages, he questioned me at length about my previous work, my academic background, and my intentions in Haiti. (Davis 1985: 46)

Davis's language is unashamedly literary. Arguing for what he sees as evidence of the African heritage in Haitian society, he describes the social environment like this:

> In the fields, long lines of men wield hoes to the rhythm of small drums, and just beyond them sit steaming pots of millet and yams ready for the harvest feast. … Markets sprout up at every crossroads, and like magnets they pull the women out of the hills; one sees their narrow traffic on the trails, the billowy walk of girls beneath baskets of rice, the silhouette of a stubborn matron dragging a half-dozen donkeys laden with eggplant. (Davis 1985: 72)

In the important section where Davis finally succeeds in meeting and encountering a man who has been made a zombi and has recovered, much of the description takes the form of dialogue between ethnographer and informant.

'Even as they cast the dirt on my coffin, I was not there. My flesh was there,' he said, pointing to the ground, 'but I floated here, moving wherever. I could hear everything that happened. Then they came. They had my soul, they called me, casting it into the ground.' Narcisse looked up from the ground. At the edge of the cemetery a pair of thin gravediggers stood as still and attentive as gazelles. Narcisse felt the weight of their recognition.

'Are they afraid of you?' Rachel asked.

'No,' he replied, 'only if I was creating problems, then I'd have problems myself.' (Davis 1985: 81)

Returning to campus in an interlude which efficiently construes the enormous gulf between rural Haiti and suburban North America, Davis presents his preliminary scientific discoveries, again largely by means of dialogue, this time with two specialists. He is now on the brink of discovering what kind of poison Haitians use to make people appear dead, but capable of being resuscitated.

'Anything on its chemistry?' [Nathan] Kline asked.

'Not much. I spoke with Professor Schultes, and he seems to think the seeds are psychoactive. He's also seen it used medicinally in Colombia to treat cholera and internal parasites.'

[Bo] Holmstedt joined in. 'There is a species of *Mucuna* called... Damn it, what is it? Yes, *flaggelipes*. It's used in Central Africa as an arrow poison.' (Davis 1985: 110)

After discussing the various possible sources of the poison, they conclude:

'What about the toad?' Holmstedt asked.

'Bufo marinus.'

'You're certain.'

'It's unmistakable. The people at Herpetology confirmed it.'

Holmstedt paused to consider. 'Quite,' he said finally, and looking straight at me. 'Wade, I'd say you're on to something.' (Davis 1985: 112)

A few pages later, Davis stumbles over the final, crucial ingredient in the Haitian concoction, namely the puffer fish. The source turns out to be an unlikely remark made by a lab worker about the final scene of a James Bond film, where it transpires that the poison prepared from this fish slows down bodily functions to the point of making people appear dead. The puzzle about the poison is resolved – the zombi phenomenon has a credible biochemical explanation – but Davis's exploration has only just begun. He now returns to Haiti determined to make sense of the dark rituals carried out by the priests of the religion of the night, to drum music and the flickering flames of torches and candles, a quest that eventually brings him to the heart of the powerful, secret Bizango society.

It is risky, to put it mildly, to present one's scientific work in this manner. Davis rarely leaves the storytelling mode to do 'proper analysis', and his own persona is so near that the reader can almost hear his voice. He never abandons the engaged, subjective viewpoint of the novice on the track of an exciting discovery. This style is not for everybody, but *The Serpent and the Rainbow* is interesting in that it shows how far one can venture from the established conventions of scientific discourse without losing caste. For the book, the ethnography and even the persona Davis has created for himself appear credible, not through the suspension of disbelief required by writers of fiction, but because of internal consistency. Davis's is not the only story told by an anthropologist about *voudon* and zombis, and it may not even be the best, but it has many strengths even if judged from an academic viewpoint. In the context of the present book, that is its most impressive achievement.

In his haunting song 'Something about Ysabel's Dance' (1989), Peter Hammill bemoans the debilitating influence of tourism on local culture ('Places disappear, but the names/remain as alibis'), but he maintains that after hours, his heroine will, maybe, 'dance the dance for real again'. The song ends with the lines, 'There's something here/the anthropologist dare not explain/Something about Ysabel's dance.' Suggesting that the academic approach is limited when it is confronted with passion, Hammill is of course right, yet he might have been impressed by Davis's optimistic, almost boyish ability to convey the flavours and smells of Haitian life without leaving his academic quest.

Now, *The Serpent and the Rainbow* arguably veers towards exoticism, but at the same time it treats Haitians respectfully and makes it possible for Western readers without much exposure to 'other cultures' to understand how and why it can be that Haitians are both different from and similar to themselves. In this shared, shrinking world of ours, anthropologists have a duty to do what they do best, namely to make credible translations between different life-worlds and world-views, and to show how such translations make embarrassing reading for global elites who see themselves as the guardians of universal humanism. Rather than regurgitating the relativist views of early twentieth-century anthropology, a contemporary public anthropology can represent a universal humanism which recognizes the significance of difference. By virtue of its experience-near material, anthropologists are in a better position than most to do this crucial job.

Let me put it like this. Asked, doubtless by an adoring disciple, about the nature of truth, the German polymath and iconoclast Rudolf Steiner responded with a counter-question: 'What is the truth about a mountain?' Responding to his own question, the ageing sage said that one could approach the mountain from the north, from the south, from the east and from the west – and, indeed, from above – and one would see different things. And one might add: one could approach the mountain with the mind of a mountaineer, a geologist, a skier, a landscape painter... So what is truth? Perhaps the most sacred contribution of European thought to world culture, one marshalled by anthropology more than any other school of thought, is the insight that all these views of the mountain are equally true and that we need a world where all the perspectives on the mountain have a rightful place. In fulfilling this vision, anthropology has an almost sacred vocation.

Targeting the Audience

As I was drafting this chapter in November 2004, I was interrupted by an e-mail from the cultural editor of the Swedish newspaper *Sydsvenska Dagbladet*, where I occasionally contribute a book review or a commentary. In the aftermath of the US elections, he wondered if, since I had written about similar topics before, I would write an article about the possible growing gulf between urban and rural populations in the North Atlantic area – not just in the US, but in Europe as well. Although the topic was not far from my field, I hesitated. After all, I had a book to finish, and the paper needed the article within a couple of days at most. On the other hand, since this book was going to be precisely about the anthropologist as public intellectual, I thought 'To hell with it', poured myself a glass of red and set to work. This is what I wrote (originally in Norwegian, translated into Swedish by *Sydsvenskan*):

Stadtluft Macht Frei

In the last couple of weeks before the US presidential elections, the media showed maps depicting the predicted outcome. Kerry was poised to win along the coasts, more specifically along the entire west coast and the east coast from Maine to Maryland. In some of the states around the Great Lakes, he was also doing well, especially in the Chicago area. The rest of the map showed a likely Republican majority. A more fine-grained map would have revealed a Democratic majority in the larger cities and Republican majorities elsewhere.

In style and external appearance, the two candidates represented different faces of the USA, and there were also marked differences in their respective political programmes. Kerry, a Yankee from the north-east, was favourable to a more visible regulation of the economy and a more responsible budget policy. He also seemed more concerned that the US should have trustworthy allies in Europe than Bush, who, on his part, carried out a rhetorically strong and emotionally potent campaign based on a particular set of ideological notions about the essential America: church and family, idyllic small-town America, and the spirit of competitiveness.

Commenting on the campaign, many have written and said that the US is a deeply divided country. [The well-known journalist] Åsne Seierstad, who covered the presidential election in Norwegian media, opined that European commentators had failed to understand 'ordinary Americans'. Most of them had supported and believed in Kerry.

Now, one may, in the name of justice, ask what makes a mechanic in the Bible belt so much more 'ordinary' than a lawyer in Boston or a student in San Francisco, and the interesting question is how the division, if it exists, can be described.

Kerry and his supporters represented the 'liberal' face of the USA (the word 'liberal', in American usage, usually means 'radical'; like 'toilet', 'radical' is a taboo word). It is the USA of the cosmopolitan big cities, the USA of multiculturalism, secular Jewry, tolerance and individualism and that of single mothers, affirmative action, tax increases and gay rights. Bush and his people stand for a more traditional modernity founded in religion, big business and petty-bourgeois values.

The distinction cannot easily be related to class. In a country where class consciousness is weakly developed, many immigrants and others in the low-income bracket vote for Bush. On the contrary, it appears to be a rural-urban contrast, which is highly interesting. It has been said time and again that Kerry is closer to Europe, culturally and ideologically, than Bush. But the truth may be that he is closer to urban Europe, that is the regions where European media commentators belong.

The maps depicting voting patterns in Norway and Sweden around the EU referendums in 1994 indicated that supporters of EU membership were in majority in the big city regions only – in and around Stockholm, Göteborg, Malmö, Oslo and Bergen. In Great Britain it has become a common view that the global city of London represents something quite different from the rest of England. And one could make a similar statement about Paris in the context of France, Berlin in Germany and Copenhagen in Denmark. The distance between city and countryside, which has been shrinking through two hundred years of determined nation-building and industrialization, seems to be growing again. This is just as true of Europe as it is of the USA.

The big cities offer much freedom and little security. They enable their inhabitants to handle dirt and complexity, noise and change. Smaller communities are more likely to cultivate their traditions and their local uniqueness. Rural belonging offers the possibility of growing roots, but one cannot grow roots through tarmac, and as a compensation, the cities offer feet.

The German saying '*Stadtluft macht frei*' [City air makes one free] has its origins in a medieval legal principle, which stated that serfs who spent more than a year in a town or city without being traced by the feudal lord, were given freedom. In more recent times, city air and freedom have been associated in other ways. Young men from the country who move to town in order to develop as individuals, are a recurrent kind of character in early modern European literature, and they are also abundantly present in African novels. The city generates complexity and makes alternative ways of life possible. I am unaware of any statistics, but I should be very surprised if gays and lesbians were not perceptibly over-represented in the big cities. Nowadays, there is a documented tendency that refugees who are forcibly placed in rural regions during the first period of their stay in Norway, move to a city as soon as their freedom of movement is returned to them.

Early twenty-first century cities are characterized by the new economy. They are no longer primarily industrial, but produce services of all kinds and enormous amounts of information. In many Western cities, there are more people paid to come up with striking slogans than there are construction workers. This tendency has led to a gentrification of European and American cities, which are currently dominated demographically by the middle classes and by ethnic minorities.

The city is associated with liberal attitudes to alternative ways of life, freedom and risk, crime and pollution, media power and multiculturalism, sinful temptations ranging from prostitution to nightclubs, coffee shops and busyness, anonymity and alienation. Many of these topics have been dealt with by writers on urban life for more than a hundred years. What is new, is the role of the big cities as nodal points in the globalization process, or 'switchboards' to use the Swedish anthropologist Ulf Hannerz's term. Here, illegal immigrants can hide and maybe find a small job without being caught by the authorities; it is in the big cities that impulses and influences from abroad first establish themselves, and it is impossible to monitor every movement and activity. The city is unruly. In Mauritius, where I lived in a fishing village for a few months, I told my host family that I intended to move to Port-Louis, the capital, about an hour's bus ride away. They warned me. Watch out for pickpockets and robbers, they said, adding that city people in general were godless and unreliable. This attitude may be typical, but the polarization between town and country is strengthened by globalization. The tendency is that city dwellers have more in common with city-dwellers in other countries than with the rural population in their own. They favour increased immigration, a weakening of religious power, free abortion, broadband, and have an international orientation.

In this tension, there is a political gulf which has not fully been exploited, but it may still come. Alain Minc wrote, in 1991, about Europe's new Middle Ages, that is alliances between cities leading to a marginalization of the urban areas, where Stockholm might have more contact with Milan than with [peripheral] Falun. The Latin of our time, the medium of communication tying the cities together, is naturally English, but Minc is too much of a Frenchman to discuss that aspect.

The big cities function like powerful magnets, but they have their limitations. For even if *Stadtluft macht frei*, it does not create security. It may seem as if the majority of American voters opted for security this time. The question is whether the same kind of polarization witnessed in the USA will also find its expression in Europe, and if so, who will win.

The form of this short article was entirely shaped by considerations about the readership. The respected culture page of *Sydsvenska Dagbladet* tends to be read by the 'chattering classes' of southern Sweden, including policymakers, academics and various others. Whenever I write anything in this newspaper, I know more specifically that it will be read by many of the academics who work at the University of Lund and Malmö University, and so writing for the paper sets me thinking, 'I wonder how my old friend O. H. is going to react to this,' or 'I'd better phrase this more carefully, since J. F. might read it'. It may well in fact be the case that, having a handful of southern Swedish readers in mind, my modest output for *Sydsvenskan* is different in tone and approach from what it would have been in a different newspaper. Such fine distinctions should not be exaggerated, but it is not a trivial point that distinct public spheres encourage distinct ways of communicating. The *New York Review of Books* review essay is a distinct genre with its own literary conventions, in-jokes and criteria for assessing quality. The 800-word book review in the *Journal of the Royal Anthropological Institute* or the *American Anthropologist* is likely to be very different from an 800-word book review published by the same reviewer, on the same book, in a daily newspaper or general-audience magazine. As editor of a bi-monthly cultural journal called *Samtiden* [The present time] from 1993 to 2001, I discovered that it would be very difficult to change the style and format of the typical *Samtiden* article. Envisioning a more experimental and varied journal when I began my tenure, I was soon to learn that when people wrote for this particular journal, they adopted a mode of writing which had developed, become associated with the journal and slowly evolved, for the last hundred years. The typical *Samtiden* article is an essay of 4,000 to 5,000 words with less than twenty endnotes and less than fifteen references, dealing with a current topic or a classical one made current through a recent event or the writer's original argument. The style of writing is light enough to be accessible to readers in their late teens, yet the content can be as challenging as the writer is capable of making it. After having received a few dozen articles of this kind, solicited and unsolicited, I began to ponder how this kind of convention could be perpetuated so efficiently. The answer is probably that the writers had a particular kind of reader in mind as they wrote, an amalgamation of the editor (whose taste was evident through the previous issues) and the ideal reader, who had probably enjoyed previous issues. While caring for one's readers is a laudable trait in any writer, stereotypical ideas about readers' expectations do not make for innovative writing. It can be a good exercise to write for different audiences, not least because it sensitizes the writer to the risk of catering to standardized formats. This risk is just as real in academic writing proper as in commercial books and journalism.

I have mentioned speed several times as a factor distinguishing typical anthropology from the typical engaged intervention. But anthropologists can write quickly if they feel they have to. Following the publication of E. O. Wilson's *Sociobiology*, Marshall Sahlins quickly wrote an angry little pamphlet, *The Use and Abuse of Biology*, denouncing Wilson's simplistic view of human life in plain language. The pamphlet did its work at the time, shifting the general focus of the debate slightly. In a situation of urgency, it can be done. It is embarrassing to observe that the commentators and analysts who set the agenda for the public buzz about global questions and geopolitics far too rarely share the intellectual approach set out at the beginning of this section, which characterize an anthropological way of thinking about the world.

Speed is not the only factor. The use of a narrative mode of presentation, good writing and a sense of urgency are equally important. Like it or not, virtually all the books on global affairs that make an impact outside academia, have a simple argument at bottom: the USA is an evil imperialist force (Chomsky); the citizens of the world want Western modernity and are embittered when they can't have it (T. Friedman, Fukuyama); there is an emerging clash of civilizations caused by fundamentally different values (Huntington); the USA is Hobbesian while Europe is Kantian (Kagan); there is a conflict between unfettered capitalism ('free markets') and democracy (Chua); the main tension in the world is between neo-liberalism and fundamentalisms (Barber). When you buy a book that signals such a message in the title or at least on the blurb, you know something about what you will get. Not everything, but enough to make you, as an interested layperson, want to pick the book up. Sahlins's hastily written pamphlet against sociobiology worked in exactly the same way. Largely dispensing with the usual academical apparatus of references, as the author admits doing at the outset, the book more than compensates for this through its temper and engagement. It is evident that something is at stake for the writer, and this kind of sentiment is contagious. It flatters us as readers because it makes us feel, just as Wade Davis does, that the writer is interested in us.

The conclusion is not that there is an inevitable trade-off between complexity and efficiency, but that narrative-driven accounts, which may in fact be engagement-driven, are more likely to catch the attention of a wide readership than chiefly analytical ones. Many anthropology books could have been turned into compelling narratives without losing their analytical complexity; the analysis would just have to be woven into the narrative. An essential voice is missing from the general intellectual debates about the state of the world – the voice which purports to say something about the view from the other side, be it remote or subaltern, or both. It is the voice of an anthropology which cares for its readers, whoever they might be.

–7–

Why Anthropology Matters

It may not be necessary that the first sentence attaches itself to the reader's eye like a fish-hook, pulling it irresistably down to the page.

But it helps if it does. I have used the project of researching and writing this book as a foil for reflecting on the ways in which anthropology could reclaim its rightful place as a fundamental intellectual discipline, and one which could contribute not only to understanding the world, but changing it. The conclusion is not a plea for populism. A massive amount of high-quality, strictly academic research is continuously being produced in anthropology, and this is not merely wonderful, but it is absolutely necessary. Yet much of this work fails to achieve the relevance it deserves, since it hardly enters into a wider ecology of ideas.

Some time ago, I came across a really nice article about the slow food movement in Italy, written by Alison Leitch for *Ethnos* (Leitch 2003). The article, or perhaps I should say essay, describes the growth of the movement as a reaction against the 'golden arches' and soulless food of the American (and domestic, it must in all justice be said) fast-food chains. The slow food movement, founded by the leftist writer and wine enthusiast Carlo Petrini in 1987 (Petrini 2001), spread quickly in certain parts of Italy in the late 1990s, and it combined a political critique of globalization-cum-standardization with a national, and often regional, patriotism associated with local produce and culinary achievement. Leitch's fieldwork area was Carrara in Tuscany, of Carrara marble fame, and following a five-year gap after her original fieldwork, she arrived to find the marble industry in a shambles, with high unemployment and general decline. Instead of continuing her fieldwork among marble workers, she was attracted to a new phenomenon, which was – of all things – the cult of lard. *Il lardo de Colonnata*, a local speciality, which has the additional charm (to some) of subverting the global low-calorie hysteria, had recently been nominated as 'the key example of a nationally "endangered food"' (Leitch 2003: 438).

What Leitch does, which makes her article so attractive, consists in tracing the shifting meaning of *lardo* through the last decades, from an unmarked local food to a potent symbol of resistance and a certain *dolce vita* associated with Italy. She also writes interestingly about the place of food in the Italian left and the inevitable conflict between local producers and the national, more highbrow Slow Food movement. It somehow reminded me of the predator debate at home in Norway, where marginal sheep-farmers want to shoot the wolves while urban conservationists want to let the endangered creatures breed in peace.

Finishing the article and wanting more, I sent Alison Leitch an e-mail asking if she had published anything about *lardo* for people who do not regularly read journals like *Ethnos*. She responded that she would love to, but well, nothing much yet. This is the situation for many of us. The reasons why most of us remain inside academia with our work include time constraints, a lack of well-developed channels outside our own closed circuits, an informal (and increasingly formal) ranking system within the subject which disdains non-academic writing, and as a consequence, a failure to develop the skills necessary to reach a larger or more varied audience.

In this book, I have spoken about the possibility of presenting the intricacies of anthropological knowledge in straightforward, vivid language, our duty to make the world simpler and more complex at the same time, and the need for a greater awareness of form and style; but I have also stressed the importance of narrative throughout. The strange lack of good stories in most anthropological writing, and the general reluctance to make bold, surprising comparisons, makes these texts tough going most of the time. Moreover, the stories and comparisons that do exist are more often than not hidden in a labyrinth of academic claptrap and discussions internal to the subject. Equally important is the consciousness about there being a public sphere out there, that there are intelligent non-specialists who care about our knowledge and who are rightfully exasperated if we fail to get it through to them.

This argument is worthwhile only because anthropology has so much to offer. Apart from providing accurate knowledge about other places and societies, it gives an appreciation of other experiences and the equal value of all human life, and not least, it helps us to understand ourselves. In the contemporary, intertwined world, anthropology should be a central part of anybody's *Bildung*, that is education in the widest sense. Anthropology can teach humility and empathy, and also the ability to listen, arguably one of the scarcest resources in the rich parts of the world these days. It can even be fun.

'You have nothing to lose but your aitches', said Orwell to his middle-class compatriots in class-divided Britain, thereby making the point that there was nothing to fear from approaching the world of the working class with an open mind. In a critical commentary on Orwell and his 'aitches', Anthony Burgess remarks: 'But those were just what he could not lose. He had at heart the cause of working-class justice, but he couldn't really accept the workers as real people' (Burgess 1978: 32–33). Unfair to Orwell as Burgess's judgement might be, it is nightmarish even to imagine that something similar might be posterity's verdict on anthropology in its twilight years of the early twenty-first century. But it is not unthinkable.

There is, in other words, a real job to be done on anthropology's relationship to the societal circulation of ideas. Even when anthropologists go out of their way to write well, to tell stories and to confront the big issues – which they sometimes do, if far too rarely – they are not noticed. It sometimes feels as though one has been pigeon holed once and for all as a dated romantic writing impenetrable texts, burnished, as it were, with the damning mark of anthropology. In this kind of situation, it is perhaps not surprising that most anthropologists retreat to their institutionalized university life. My view, which has been made apparent throughout this short book, is that we should do the opposite, that anthropology needs a PR strategy, both for the sake of the enlightenment of the world and for the future of the discipline.

Seen from the perspective of the interested and enlightened layperson, scientific research can be likened to a space mission. One sends a probe into space, ceremoniously waving it off in the anticipation that it will return with new knowledge about the universe. Each time one such spacecraft fails to return, but instead chooses to stay out there, pondering the calm darkness in silence, it becomes less likely that our enlightened citizen will contribute funds for another probe. If the world is our oyster, our job is to make it talk.

Bibliography

Ahmed, Akbar S. (1992) *Islam and Postmodernism: Predicament and Promise*. London: Routledge.

—— and Cris Shore (eds) (1995) *The Future of Anthropology: Its Relevance to the Contemporary World*. London: Athlone.

American Anthropological Association (1947) Statement on Human Rights. *American Anthropologist*, **49** (4): 539–43.

Ardener, Edwin (1985) 'The end of modernism in social anthropology', in *Reason and Morality*, (ed.) Joanna Overing, pp. 47–70. London: Tavistock.

Aunger, Robert (2002) *The Electric Meme: A new Theory of How We Think*. New York: Free Press.

—— (2000) (ed.) *Darwinizing Culture: The Status of Memetics as a Science*. Oxford: Oxford University Press.

Barber, Benjamin (1996) *Jihad vs. McWorld: How Globalism and Tribalism are Reshaping the World*. New York: Ballantine.

Barley, Nigel (1985) *The Innocent Anthropologist. Notes from a Mud Hut*. Harmondsworth: Penguin.

Barnard, Alan (1999) 'Modern hunter-gatherers and early symbolic culture', in *The Evolution of Culture: An Interdisciplinary View*, (eds) Chris Knight, Robin Dunbar and Camilla Powers, pp. 50–70. Edinburgh: Edinburgh University Press.

Barth, Fredrik (1980) *Andres Liv – og Vårt Eget* [Others' Lives – and Our Own]. Oslo: Gyldendal.

—— (1969) (ed.) *Ethnic Groups and Boundaries: The Social Organization of Culture Difference*. Oslo: Scandinavian University Press.

Bateson, Gregory (1972) 'Ecology and flexibility in urban civilization', in Bateson, *Steps to an Ecology of Mind*, pp. 502–514. New York: Basic Books.

—— (1978) *Mind and Nature*. Glasgow: Fontana.

Baumann, Gerd (1996) *Contesting Culture: Discourses of Identity in Multi-ethnic London*. Cambridge: Cambridge University Press.

Benedict, Ruth 1970 [1934] *Patterns of Culture*. Boston, MA: Houghton Mifflin.

—— 1974 [1946] *The Chrysanthemum and the Sword*. Boston, MA: Houghton Mifflin.

Benthall, Jonathan (2002a) General introduction, in *The Best of Anthropology Today*, (ed.) Jonathan Benthall, pp. 1–15. London: Routledge.

—— (2002b) (ed.) *The Best of Anthropology Today*. London: Routledge.

Berlin, Isaiah (1976) *Vico and Herder. Two studies in the history of ideas*. London: Hogarth Press.

Berreman, Gerald (1968) 'Is anthropology alive?', in *Current Anthropology* **9** (5): 391–396.

Blackmore, Susan (1999) *The Meme Machine*. Oxford: Oxford University Press.

Bloch, Maurice (2000) 'A well-disposed anthropologist's problems with memes', in *Darwinizing Culture*, (ed.) Robert Aunger, pp. 189–204. Oxford: Oxford University Press.

Borchgrevink, Tordis (2003) 'Et ubehag i antropologien' [Something unsettling in anthropology], in *Nære Steder, Nye Rom: Utfordringer i Antropologiske Studier i Norge* [Close Places, New Spaces: Challenges for Anthropological Studies in Norway], (eds) Marianne Rugkåsa and Kari T. Thorsen, pp. 263–291. Oslo: Gyldendal.

Borofsky, Robert (2005) *Yanomami: The Fierce Controversy and What We Can Learn From It*. Berkeley: University of California Press.

Boskovic, Aleksandar (2003) 'Phantoms of Africa: Michel Leiris and the anthropology of the continent', in *Gradhiva* **34**: 1–6.

Bourgois, Philip (2002) 'Understanding inner-city poverty: Resistance and self-destruction under US apartheid', in *Exotic No More*, (ed.) Jeremy MacClancy, pp. 15–32. Chicago: University of Chicago Press.

Bringa, Tone (1996) *Being Muslim the Bosnian way: Identity and Community in a Central Bosnian Village*. Princeton, NJ: Princeton University Press.

Brockman, John (1995) (ed.) *The Third Culture: Beyond the Scientific Revolution*. New York: Simon & Schuster.

Burgess, Anthony (1978) *1985*. London: Hutchinson.

Çaglar, Ayse (1999) 'McKebap: Döner kebap and the social positioning struggle of German Turks', in *Changing Food Habits: Case Studies from Africa, South America and Europe*, (ed.) Carola Lentz, pp. 263–283. Amsterdam: Harwood.

Campbell, Alan (1996) 'Tricky tropes: Styles of the popular and the pompous', in *Popularizing Anthropology*, (eds) Jeremy MacClancy and Chris McDonaugh, pp. 58–82. London: Routledge.

Carrithers, Michael (1992) *Why Humans have Cultures: Explaining Anthropology and Social Diversity*. Oxford: Oxford University Press.

Castells, Manuel (1996) *The Rise of the Network Society*. (The Information Society, I) Oxford: Blackwells.

Chagnon, Napoleon (1983) *Yanomamö. The Fierce People*, 3rd edition. New York: Holt, Rinehart & Winston.

Chua, Amy (2003) *World on Fire: How Exporting Free Market Democracy Breeds Ethnic Hatred and Global Instability*. London: Arrow.

Clastres, Pierre (1977) *La Société Contre l'État*. Paris: Minuit.

—— (1988) Society Against the State, trans. Paul Auster. New York: Zone Books.

Clifford, James (1997) *Routes. Travel and Translation in the Late Twentieth Century*. Cambridge: Harvard University Press.

—— and George Marcus (1986) (eds) *Writing Culture: The Poetics and Politics of Ethnography.* Berkeley: University of California Press.

Cohen, Abner (1981) *The Politics of Elite Culture: Explorations in the Dramaturgy of Power in a Modern African Society.* Berkeley: University of California Press.

—— (1993) *Masquerade Politics: Explorations in the Structure of Urban Cultural Movements.* Berkeley: University of California Press.

Crapanzano, Vincent (1980) *Tuhami: Portrait of a Moroccan.* Chicago: University of Chigaco Press.

Darwin, Charles (1981 [1871]) *The Descent of Man, and Selection in Relation to Sex.* Princeton: Princeton University Press.

Davis, Wade (1985) *The Serpent and the Rainbow.* London: Collins.

Dawkins, Richard (1976) *The Selfish Gene.* Oxford: Oxford University Press.

—— (1986) *The Blind Watchmaker.* London: Longman.

—— (2004) 'Race and creation', in *Prospect,* **103** (October 2004).

Deloria, Vine Jr. (1969) *Custer Died for your Sins: An Indian Manifesto.* New York: Macmillan.

Dennett, Daniel (1995) *Darwin's Dangerous Idea: Evolution and the Meanings of Life.* New York: Simon & Schuster.

Descola, Philippe (1996) 'A *bricoleur*'s workshop: Writing *Les Lances du Crépuscule*', in *Popularizing Anthropology,* (eds) Jeremy MacClancy and Chris McDonaugh, pp. 208–224. London: Routledge.

Diamond, Jared (1997) *Guns, Germs and Steel: A Short History of Everyone for the Last 13,000 Years.* London: Jonathan Cape.

—— (2005) *Collapse: How Societies Choose to Fail or Succeed.* London: Allen Lane.

di Leonardo, Micaela (1998) *Exotics at Home: Anthropologies, Others, American Modernity.* Chicago: University of Chicago Press.

—— (2001) 'Margaret Mead vs. Tony Soprano', in *The Nation,* May 21, 2001.

Donner, Florinda (1992) *Shabono.* San Francisco: Harper.

Douglas, Mary (1966) *Purity and Danger.* London: Routledge & Kegan Paul.

Døving, Runar (2004) *Rype med Lettøl* [Grouse with Light Beer]. Oslo: Pax.

Duerr, Hans Peter (1984) *Sedna oder die Liebe zum Leben.* Frankfurt-am-Main: Suhrkamp.

Eriksen, Thomas Hylland (1996) Counterreactions: 'No to EU' and the FIS in the eye of the whirlwind of global modernity. http://folk.uio.no/geirthe/Counterreactions.html

—— (2001a) *Bak Fiendebildet: Islam og Verden etter 11. September* [Behind the Enemy Image: Islam and the World after 11 September]. Oslo: Cappelen.

—— (2001b) *Tyranny of the Moment: Fast and Slow Time in the Information Age.* London: Pluto.

—— (2003a) 'Antropologien og den offentlige debatt' [Anthropology and public debate], in *Nære Steder, Nye Rom: Utfordringer i Antropologiske Studier i Norge*

[Close Places, New Spaces: Challenges for Anthropological Studies in Norway], (eds) Marianne Rugkåsa and Kari T. Thorsen, pp. 292–313. Oslo: Gyldendal.

—— (2003b) 'The young rebel and the dusty professor: A tale of anthropologists and the media in Norway', in *Anthropology Today*, **19** (1): 3–5.

Evans-Pritchard, E. E. (1951) *Social Anthropology*. London: Cohen & West.

Firth, Rosemary (1984) 'Anthropology in fiction: An image of fieldwork', in *RAIN*, **64**: 7–9.

Foucault, Michel (2001) *Fearless Speech*, (ed.) Joseph Pearson. New York: Semiotext(e).

Fox, Kate (2004) *Watching the English: The Hidden Rules of English Behaviour*. London: Hodder & Stoughton.

Freeman, Derek (1983) *Margaret Mead and Samoa: The Making and Unmaking of an Anthropological Myth*. Cambridge, MA: Harvard University Press.

Friedman, Jonathan (1997) 'Global crises, the struggle for cultural identity and intellectual porkbarrelling: Cosmopolitans versus locals, ethnics and nationals in an era of de-hegemonisation', in *Debating Cultural Hybridity: Multi-cultural Identities and the Politics of Anti-racism*, (eds) Tariq Modood and Pnina Werbner, pp. 70–89. London: Zed.

Friedman, Thomas (1999) *The Lexus and the Olive Tree*. New York: Farrar, Strauss & Giroux.

Fukuyama, Francis (1993) *The end of History and the Last Man*. New York: Avon.

Furedi, Frank (2004) *Where Have all the Intellectuals Gone? Confronting 21st-Century Philistinism*. London: Continuum.

Gardner, Katy (1997) *Songs from River's Edge: Stories from a Bangladeshi Village*. London: Pluto.

—— (2002) *Losing Gemma*. London: Penguin.

Geertz, Clifford (1973) *The Interpretation of Cultures*. New York: Basic Books.

—— (1998) 'Deep hanging out', in *New York Review of Books*, **45** (16): 69–72.

Gellner, Ernest (1991) *Reason and Culture: The Historical Role of Rationality and Rationalism*. Oxford: Blackwell.

Gillespie, Marie (1995) *Television, Ethnicity and Cultural Change*. London: Routledge.

González, Roberto J. (2004) (ed.) *Anthropologists in the Public Sphere: Speaking Out on War, Peace and American Power*. Austin: University of Texas Press.

Goody, Jack (1995) *The Expansive Moment: Anthropology in Britain and Africa 1918–1970*. Cambridge: Cambridge University Press.

—— and Ian Watt (1963) 'The consequences of literacy', in *Comparative Studies in Society and History*, **5**: 304–345.

Gould, Stephen Jay (2002) *The Structure of Evolutionary Theory*. Cambridge, MA: Belknap.

—— and Elizabeth Vrba (1981) 'Exaptation: A missing term in the science of form', in *Paleobiology*, **8**: 4–15.

Gray, John (2000) *Two Faces of Liberalism*. Cambridge: Polity.

Greene, Graham (1965) *The Comedians*. London: Bodley Head.

Grillo, Ralph (1994) 'The application of anthropology in Britain, 1983–1993', in *When History Accelerates*, (ed.) Chris Hann, pp. 300–316. London: Athlone.

Grimshaw, Anna and Keith Hart (1993) *Anthropology and the Crisis of the Intellectuals*. Cambridge: Prickly Pear Press (Prickly Pear Pamphlet no. 1).

Gullestad, Marianne (1996) *Everyday Philosophers: Modernity, Morality and Autobiography in Norway*. Oslo: Universitetsforlaget.

—— (2002) *Det Norske sett med Nye Øyne* [Norwegianness in a new perspective]. Oslo: Universitetsforlaget.

—— (2003) 'Kunnskap for hvem?' [Knowledge for whom?], in *Nære Steder, Nye Rom: Utfordringer i Antropologiske Studier i Norge* [Close Places, New Spaces: Challenges for Anthropological Studies in Norway], (eds) Marianne Rugkåsa and Kari T. Thorsen, pp. 233–262. Oslo: Gyldendal.

Habermas, Jürgen (1968) *Erkenntnis und Interesse*. Frankfurt-am-Main: Suhrkamp.

Hannerz, Ulf (1992) *Cultural Complexity*. New York: Columbia University Press.

—— (2003) *Foreign News: Exploring the World of Foreign Correspondents*. Chicago: University of Chicago Press.

—— (2004a) 'Introduktion: Mellan två skrivarkulturer' [Introduction: Between two cultures of writing], in *Antropologi/journalistik*, (ed.) Ulf Hannerz, pp. 5–37. Lund: Studentlitteratur.

—— (2004b) (ed.) *Antropologi/journalistik: Om Sätt att Beskriva Världen* [Anthropology/journalism: On Ways to Describe the World]. Lund: Studentlitteratur.

Harris, Marvin (1978) *Cannibals and Kings: The Origins of Culture*. Glasgow: Fontana.

—— (1987) *Why Nothing Works: The Anthropology of Everyday Life*. New York: Simon & Schuster.

Hart, Keith (2000) *The Memory Bank: Money in an Unequal World*. London: Profile.

—— (2003) 'British social anthropology's nationalist project', in *Anthropology Today*, **19** (6): 1–2.

Heath, S. B. (1983) *Ways with Words: Language, Life and Work in Communities and Classrooms*. Cambridge: Cambridge University Press.

Hellman, Harold (1996) *Great Feuds in Science: Ten of the Liveliest Disputes Ever*. London: Wiley.

Hendry, Joy (1996) 'The chrysanthemum continues to flower: Ruth Benedict and some perils of popular anthropology', in *Popularizing Anthropology*, (eds) Jeremy MacClancy and Chris McDonaugh, pp. 106–121. London: Routledge.

Holmes, Douglas R. (2000) *Integral Europe: Fast-capitalism, Multiculturalism, Neo-fascism*. Oxford: Princeton University Press.

Huntington, Samuel (1996) *The Clash of Civilizations and the Remaking of a World Order*. New York: Simon and Schuster

138 • *Bibliography*

Ingold, Tim (1986) *Evolution and Social Life*. Cambridge: Cambridge University
Press.
—— (2000) *The Perception of the Environment. Essays in Livelihood, Dwelling and
Skill*. London: Routledge.
—— (1996) (ed.) *Key Debates in Anthropology*. London: Routledge.
Jacoby, Russell (1987) *The Last Intellectuals: American Culture in the Age of
Academe*. New York: Basic Books.
Jencks, Charles (2001) 'EP, phone home', in *Alas Poor Darwin*, (eds) Hilary Rose
and Steven Rose, pp. 28–46. London: Vintage.
Jones, Steve (1997) *In the Blood: God, Genes and Destiny*. London: Flamingo.
Kaplan, Robert (1997) *The Ends of the Earth*. New York: Fodor.
Kearney, Michael (2004) *Changing Fields of Anthropology: From Local to Global*.
Oxford: Rowman & Littlefield.
Klausen, Arne Martin (1984) (ed.) *Den Norske Væremåten* [The Norwegian Way of
Being]. Oslo: Cappelen.
—— (1999) (ed.) *Olympic Games as Performance and Public Event: The Case of
the XVII Winter Olympic Games in Norway*. New York: Berghahn.
Klein, Naomi (1999) *No Space, No Choice, No Jobs, No Logo: Taking Aim at the
Brand Bullies*. New York: Picador.
Knight, Chris, Robin Dunbar and Camilla Powers (1999) 'An evolutionary approach
to human culture', in Robin Dunbar, Chris Knight and Camilla Powers (eds), *The
Evolution of Culture*. Edinburgh: Edinburgh University Press.
Kohn, Marek (1999) *As We Know It. Coming to Terms with an Evolved Mind*.
London: Granta.
Kuper, Adam (1988) *The Invention of Primitive Society*. London: Routledge.
—— (1994) *The Chosen Primate: Human Nature and Cultural Diversity*. Cambridge,
MA: Harvard University Press.
—— (1996) *Anthropology and Anthropologists: The Modern British School*. London:
Routledge.
—— (1999) *Culture: The Anthropologist's Account*. Cambridge, MA: Harvard
University Press.
—— (2000) 'If memes are the answer, what is the question?', in *Darwinizing
Culture*, (ed.) Robert Aunger, pp. 175–188. Oxford: Oxford University Press.
Kurkiala, Mikael (2003) 'Interpreting honour killings: The story of Fadime Sahindal
(1975–2002) in the Swedish press', in *Anthropology Today*, **19** (1): 6–7.
Leach, Edmund (1970) *Claude Lévi-Strauss*. New York: Viking.
—— (1973) 'Keep social anthropology out of the curriculum', in *Times Educational
Supplement*, Feb 2: 4.
Leiris, Michel (1981 [1934]) *L'Afrique Fantôme*. Paris: Gallimard.
Leitch, Alison (2003) 'Slow food and the politics of pork fat: Italian food and
European identity', in *Ethnos* **68** (4): 437–462.
Lévi-Strauss, Claude (1949) *Les Structures Élémentaires de la Parenté*. Paris: PUF.

—— (1962) *La Pensée Sauvage*. Paris: Plon.

—— (1968) *Les Origines des Manières du Table*. Mythologiques III. Paris: Plon.

—— (1978a [1955]) *Tristes Tropiques*. Harmondsworth: Penguin.

—— (1978b) *Myth and Meaning*. London: Routledge and Kegan Paul.

—— (1988) *De Près et de Loin*, with Didier Eribon. Paris: Odile Jacob

Linton, Ralph (1936) *The Study of Man: An Introduction*. New York: Appleton-Century.

—— (1937) 'One Hundred Per Cent American', in *The American Mercury* **40**: 427–429.

Louch, Alfred R. (1966) *Explanation and Human Action*. Oxford: Blackwell.

Löfving, Staffan (2004) 'Om krigets konturer' [On the outlines of war], in *Antropologi/ journalistik*, (ed.) Ulf Hannerz, pp. 115–142. Lund: Studentlitteratur.

MacClancy, Jeremy (1996) 'Popularizing anthropology', in *Popularizing Anthropology*, (eds) Jeremy MacClancy and Chris McDonaugh, pp. 1–57. London: Routledge.

—— (2004) (ed.) *Exotic No More: Anthropology on the Front Lines*. Chicago: University of Chicago Press.

—— and Chris McDonaugh (eds) (1996) *Popularizing Anthropology*. London: Routledge.

Macfarlane, Alan (2005) *Letters to Lily: On How the World Works*. London: Profile.

Mahmoody, Betty (1989) *Not Without My Daughter*. New York: Corgi.

Malik, Kenan (2000) *Man, Beast, or Zombie: What Science Can and Cannot Tell Us About Human Nature*. London: Weidenfeld & Nicholson.

—— (2005) 'Islamophobia myth', in *Prospect* 107 (February 2005): 24–28.

Malinowski, Bronislaw (1984 [1922]) *Argonauts of the Western Pacific*. Prospect Heights: Waveland.

Malkki, Liisa (1995) *Purity and Exile: Violence, Memory, and National Cosmology among Hutu Refugees in Tanzania*. Chicago: University of Chicago Press.

Marcus, Geoge E. (1999) *Ethnography Through Thick and Thin*. Princeton: Princeton University Press.

—— and Michael M. J. Fischer (1986) *Anthropology as Cultural Critique: An Experimental Moment in the Human Sciences*. Chicago: University of Chicago Press.

Mauss, Marcel (1954 [1924]) *The Gift*. London: Cohen & West.

—— (1960/1934) 'Les techniques du corps', in Mauss, *Sociologie et Anthropologie*. Paris: PUF.

Maybury-Lewis, David (1992) *Millennium: Tribal Wisdom and the Modern World*. London: Viking.

McLuhan, Marshall (1994 [1964]) *Understanding Media*. London: Routledge.

Mead, Margaret (1930) *Growing Up in New Guinea: A Comparative Study of Primitive Education*. New York: The American Library.

—— (1977 [1928]) *Coming of Age in Samoa*. Harmondsworth: Penguin.

—— (1950 [1935]) *Sex and Temperament in Three Primitive Societies*. New York: Mentor.

Midgley, Mary (2001) 'Why memes?', in *Alas Poor Darwin*, (eds) Hilary Rose and Steven Rose, pp. 67–84. London: Jonathan Cape.

Miller, Daniel (1998) *A Theory of Shopping*. Cambridge: Polity.

—— (2001) *The Dialectics of Shopping*. Chicago: University of Chicago Press.

—— and Mukulika Banerjee (2003) *The Sari*. Oxford: Berg.

Mills, C. Wright (1980 [1959]) *The Sociological Imagination*. Harmondsworth: Penguin.

Mills, David (2003) 'Professionalizing or popularizing anthropology?', in *Anthropology Today*, **19** (5): 8–13.

Mimouni, Rachid (1992) *De la Barbarie en Général et de l'Intégrisme en Particulier*. Paris: Le Pré aux Clercs.

Minc, Alain (1993) *Le Nouveau Moyen Âge*. Paris: Broché.

Miner, Horace (1956) 'Body Ritual among the Nacirema', in *American Anthropologist*, **58**: 503–507.

Montagu, Ashley (1997 [1942]) *Man's Most Dangerous Idea: The Fallacy of Race*, 6th rev. edition. Walnut Creek: AltaMira.

—— (1952) 'The "Go-Getter" Spirit: Competition thrives on insecurity, works against democracy'. http://www.harvardsquarelibrary.org/unitarians/montagu. html. Originally published in *The Christian Register*, November 1952.

Morin, Edgar (2001) *L'Identité Humaine* (La Méthode V). Paris: Seuil.

Morphy, Howard (1996) 'Proximity and distance: representations of Aboriginal society in the writings of Bill Harney and Bruce Chatwin', in *Popularizing Anthropology*, (eds) Jeremy MacClancy and Chris McDonaugh, pp. 157–179. London: Routledge.

Morris, Brian (1994) *Anthropology of the Self*. London: Pluto.

Myhre, Knut Christian (2004) 'The bookseller of Kabul and the anthropologists of Norway', in *Anthropology Today*, **20** (3): 19–22.

Neumann, Iver B. (2004) 'Maktkritikk som antropologiens adelsmerke' [Critique of power as defining trait of anthropology], in *Norsk Antropologisk Tidsskrift*, **15**: 133–144.

Nørretranders, Tor (1999) *The User Illusion*. Harmondsworth: Penguin.

Olwig, Karen Fog (2003) 'Global places and place-identities – lessons from Caribbean research', in *Globalization – Studies in Anthropology*, (ed.) T. H. Eriksen, pp. 58–77. London: Pluto.

Ong, Aihwa (1999) *Flexible Citizenship: The Cultural Logics of Transnationality*. Durham: Duke University Press.

Pamuk, Orhan (2004) *Snow*. London: Faber & Faber.

Peterson, Mark Allen (1991) 'Aliens, ape men and wacky savages: the anthropologist in the tabloids', in *Anthropology Today*, 7:5.

Petrini, Carlo (2001) *Slow Food: The Case for Taste*. New York: Columbia University Press.

Pinker, Steven (1994) *The Language Instinct*. London: Allen Lane.

—— (2002) *The Blank Slate: The Modern Denial of Human Nature*. London: Penguin.

Pratt, Mary Louise (1986) 'Fieldwork in common places', in *Writing Culture. The Poetics and Politics of Ethnography*, (eds) James Clifford and George Marcus, pp. 27–50. Berkeley: University of California Press.

Putnam, Robert (2001) *Bowling Alone: The Collapse and Revival of American Community*. New York: Simon & Schuster.

Reddy, G. Prakash (1993) *'Danes Are Like That!' Perspectives of an Indian Anthropologist on the Danish Society*. Mørke: Grevas.

Ridley, Matt (1996) *The Origins of Virtue: Human Instincts and the Evolution of Cooperation*. London: Viking.

Ritzer, George (2000/1993) *The McDonaldization of Society*, millennium edition. Thousand Oaks: Pine Forge Press.

Robin, Ron (2004) *Scandals and Scoundrels: Seven Cases that Shook the Academy*. Berkeley: University of California Press.

Rose, Steven (1996) *Lifelines: Biology Beyond Determinism*. Oxford: Oxford University Press.

Rose, Hilary and Steven Rose (eds) (2001) *Alas Poor Darwin: Arguments Against Evolutionary Psychology*. London: Jonathan Cape.

Rugkåsa, Marianne and Kari T. Thorsen, (eds) (2003) *Nære Steder, Nye Rom: Utfordringer i Antropologiske Studier i Norge* [Close Places, New Spaces: Challenges for Anthropological Studies in Norway]. Oslo: Gyldendal.

Sahlins, Marshall (1972) *Stone Age Economics*. Chicago: Aldine.

—— (1977) *The Use and Abuse of Biology*. Chicago: University of Chicago Press.

—— (1993) *Waiting for Foucault*. London: Prickly Pear Press (Prickly Pear Pamphlet #3).

—— (1999) 'Two or three things that I know about culture', in *Journal of the Royal Anthropological Institute*, 5: 399–422.

Said, Edward W. (1993) *Representations of the Intellectual*. London: Vintage.

Salemink, Oscar (2003) *The Ethnography of Vietnam's Central Highlanders: A Historical Contextualization 1850–1990*. London: Routledge/Curzon.

Scheper-Hughes, Nancy (1979) *Saints, Scholars and Schizophrenics: Mental Illness in Rural Ireland*. Berkelely: University of California Press.

—— (1992) *Death Without Weeping: The violence of Everyday Life in Brazil*. Berkeley: University of California Press.

Schneider, Jane (1994) 'In and out of polyester: Desire, disdain and global fibre competitions', in *Anthropology Today*, **10** (4): 2–10.

Scribner, Sylvia and Michael Cole (1981) *The Psychology of Literacy*. Cambridge, MA: Harvard University Press.

Seierstad, Åsne (2004) *The Bookseller of Kabul*. London: Virago.

Semon, Richard (1908) *Die Mneme als Erhaltendes Prinzip in Wechsel des Organizchen Geschehens*. Leipzig: Wilhelm Engelmann.

Shore, Cris (1996) 'Anthropology's identity crisis', in *Anthropology Today*, **12** (2): 2–5.

Shostak, Marjorie (1981) *Nisa: the Life and Words of an !Kung Woman*. Cambridge: Harvard University Press.

Spencer, Jonathan (2000) 'British social anthropology: A retrospective', in *Annual Review of Anthropology*, **29**; 1–24.

Sperber, Dan (2000) 'An objection to the memetic approach to culture', in *Darwinizing Culture*, (ed.) Robert Aunger, pp. 163–174. Oxford: Oxford University Press.

—— and Deirdre Wilson (1986) *Relevance: Communication and Cognition*. Oxford: Blackwells.

Stewart, Charles (1992) 'The popularization of anthropology', in *Anthropology Today*, **8** (4): 15–16.

Steinick, Karl (2004) 'Den rätta vinkeln: Geojournalistik och hjärtekrossarantropologi' [The right angle: Global journalism and heartbreaking anthropology], in *Antropologi/journalistik*, (ed.) Ulf Hannerz, pp. 183–212. Lund: Studentlitteratur.

Stocking, George W. Jr. (1992) *The Ethnographer's Magic and other Essays in the History of Anthropology*. Madison: University of Wisconsin Press.

Strathern, Marilyn (1988) *The Gender of the Gift: Problems with Women and Problems with Society in Melanesia*. Cambridge: Cambridge University Press.

—— (1992) *Reproducing the Future: Anthropology, Kinship and the New Reproductive Technologies*. Manchester: Manchester University Press.

Sutton, David (1991) 'Is anybody out there? Anthropology and the question of audience', in *Critique of Anthropology*, **11** (1): 91–104.

Talle, Aud (2003) *Om Kvinneleg Omskjering* [On Female Circumcision]. Oslo: Samlaget.

Tierney, Patrick (2000) *Darkness in El Dorado: How Scientists and Journalists Devastated the Amazon*. New York: Norton.

Todorov, Tzvetan (2000) *Mémoire du Mal, Tentation du Bien: Enquête sur le Siècle*. Paris: Robert Laffont.

Tooby, John and Leda Cosmides (1992) 'The psychological foundations of Culture', in *The Adapted Mind: Evolutionary Psychology and the Generation of Culture*, (eds) Jerome Barkow, Leda Cosmides and John Tooby, pp. 19–136. Oxford: Oxford University Press.

Turnbull, Colin (1961) *The Forest People*. New York: Simon & Schuster.

—— (1972) *The Mountain People*. London: Jonathan Cape.

Turner, Terence (1993) 'Multiculturalism and anthropology', in *Cultural Anthropology*, **8** (4): 411–429.

Turner, Victor (1969) *The Ritual Process*. Chicago: Aldine.

de Waal, Alex (1989) *Famine that Kills: Darfur, Sudan, 1984–1985*. Oxford: Clarendon.

White, Leslie (1948) 'Man's control over civilization: An anthropocentric illusion', in *The Scientific Monthly*, **66**: 235–247.

Whitehouse, Harvey (2001) (ed.) *The Debated Mind: Evolutionary Psychology Versus Ethnography*. Oxford: Berg.

Wikan, Unni (1980) *Life Among the Poor in Cairo*. London: Tavistock.

—— (1995) *Mot en Ny Norsk Underklasse?* [Towards a new Norwegian Underclass?] Oslo: Gyldendal.

—— (2001) *Generous Betrayal*. Chicago: University of Chicago Press.

Wilken, Patrick (1994) *Anthropology, the Intellectuals and the Gulf War*. Cambridge: Prickly Pear Press (Prickly Pear Pamphlet # 5).

Wilson, Edward O. (1975) *Sociobiology: The New Synthesis*. Cambridge, MA: Harvard University Press.

—— (1978) *On Human Nature*. Cambridge, MA: Harvard University Press.

Wilson, Peter J. (1978) *Crab Antics*, 2nd edition. New Haven, CT: Yale University Press.

—— (1980) *Man – the Promising Primate: The Conditions of Human Evolution*. New Haven: Yale University Press.

Wogan, Peter (2004) 'Deep hanging out: Reflections on fieldwork and multi-sited Andean ethnography', in *Identities*, **11**: 129–139.

Wolf, Eric (1982) *Europe and the People Without History*. Berkeley: University of California Press.

Worsley, Peter (1984) *The Three Worlds. Culture and World Development*. London: Weidenfeld & Nicholson.

Zizek, Slavoj (2000) *The Ticklish Subject*. London: Verso.

Index